PROBLEMS IN WRITTEN EXPRESSION
Assessment and Remediation

The Guilford School Practitioner Series

EDITORS

STEPHEN N. ELLIOTT, Ph.D.
University of Wisconsin—Madison

JOSEPH C. WITT, Ph.D.
Louisiana State University, Baton Rouge

Academic Skills Problems: Direct Assessment and Intervention
EDWARD S. SHAPIRO

Curriculum-Based Measurement: Assessing Special Children
MARK R. SHINN (ED.)

Suicide Intervention in the Schools
SCOTT POLAND

Problems in Written Expression: Assessment and Remediation
SHARON BRADLEY-JOHNSON AND JUDI LUCAS LESIAK

PROBLEMS IN WRITTEN EXPRESSION
Assessment and Remediation

SHARON BRADLEY-JOHNSON, Ed.D.
JUDI LUCAS LESIAK, Ph.D.
Central Michigan University

THE GUILFORD PRESS
New York   London

120741

© 1989 The Guilford Press
A Division of Guilford Publications, Inc.
72 Spring Street, New York, NY 10012

Printed in the United States of America

This book is printed on acid-free paper.

Last digit is print number: 9 8 7 6 5 4 3 2 1

Library of Congress Cataloging-in-Publication Data
Bradley-Johnson, Sharon.
  Problems in written expression: assessment and remediation.

  (The Guilford school practitioner series)
  Bibliography: p.
  Includes index.
  1. Language arts—Ability testing.   2. English language—Composition and exercises—Ability testing. 3. Language arts—Remedial teaching.   I. Lesiak, Judi. II. Title.   III. Series: Guilford school practitioner series.
  LB1576.B574   1988   428'.0076   88-32830
  ISBN 0-89862-354-5
  ISBN 0-89862-233-6 (soft)

Contents

PROBLEMS IN WRITTEN EXPRESSION
Assessment and Remediation

1

Introduction

All writing is communication.
William Strunk and E. B. White (1972, p. 60)

IMPORTANCE OF WRITTEN EXPRESSION SKILLS

Skills in written expression are necessary for students to make adequate academic progress. As students move through the school system, especially into junior high and high school, more and more writing is required on tests and papers. Writing skills also are required to varying degrees in different jobs. Further, written expression is a vehicle for sharing feelings and thoughts with others. Thus, the importance of written expression cannot be overemphasized.

Until recently, however, this area has received relatively little attention from educators and psychologists compared with other academic areas such as reading and mathematics. Until written expression was included as a category for learning disabilities in Public Law (PL) 94-142, the assessment of written expression tended to focus primarily—or only—on spelling. The relative lack of attention in terms of research, test development, and curriculum development is unfortunate. However, it is not surprising that such an important area has been ignored, given the complexity of this method of communication.

COMPONENTS OF WRITTEN EXPRESSION

The majority of authors who address written expression note that writing is one of humanity's highest achievements because it requires the integration of many skills. Larsen (1987) suggests that there are

1

five skill areas, or components, that are important for written expression: (1) mechanics, (2) production, (3) conventions, (4) linguistics, and (5) cognition.

Mechanics refers to a student's ability to form letters, words, numbers, and sentences that are legible; in other words, the student's handwriting. Larsen (1987) points out that handwriting must at least be serviceable; otherwise, the content of what is written will not be conveyed to the reader. The production aspect of written expression, that is, the number of words, sentences, and paragraphs a student is able to generate, is important to convey ideas and feelings with sufficient support and to produce a product of good quality. Conventions consist of the rules for capitalization, punctuation, and spelling. Hammill and Bartel (1982) note that many of the rules for capitalization and punctuation "are arbitrary in nature, based in tradition, and do not necessarily facilitate meaning" (p. 3). However, if a student has problems with these rules, or the rules for correct spelling, the written product may not be of good quality and may be difficult or even impossible to understand.

The linguistic component consists of the ability to use varied vocabulary and correct syntax. Skills in this area are a function of the student's oral language development. As Larsen (1987) suggests, the rules involved are often arbitrary, as with the rules for conventions. Material written using incorrect grammar and vocabulary is not acceptable in classrooms because it makes the writer appear to be not well educated. The cognitive component of written expression refers to the organizational aspect, that is, whether the product is logical, sequential, and coherent. As with the other components, problems with this component not only affect the quality of the written product, but also can make the writing difficult or impossible to understand.

Each of these components of written expression is built on other complex skills. For example, handwriting, the earliest component taught, requires the ability to imitate, coordination of vision and motor abilities, and accurate memory. Performance in the linguistic area is directly tied to skills in oral language. The use of conventions requires the student to pay close attention to detail.

In addition, all five components are interrelated. Thus, a problem with one component will be likely to result in difficulty with one or more of the other components. For example, if a student has problems with spelling, this may limit the vocabulary used in writing to only those words the student feels confident about spelling. Thus, the complex nature of written expression makes it a difficult academic area; the complexity also makes assessment, remediation, and research in this area difficult and time-consuming.

The emphasis of this book is on assessment of the first four components: mechanics, production, conventions, and linguistics. Though assessment and remediation of the cognitive aspect will be addressed, in-depth discussion of this component is limited at the present time by a lack of clarity regarding what cognitive skills are involved; also, there are few tests and little remedial material available for this aspect of written expression.

DIFFICULTIES IN ASSESSMENT

Examiners often have had difficulty assessing the written expression skills of students. In addition to the complex nature of writing, another factor that complicates assessment and remediation is the lack of consensus among professionals regarding which specific skills are needed for school success. While most professionals agree on the skills involved in the mechanics and conventions of writing, there is still debate about the skills that are critical for linguistics or cognition. Until these skills are delineated, assessment and remediation will be difficult.

However, within the past few years, research has increased, and the number and quality of assessment instruments and curricular materials have increased. This change has provided examiners and teachers with more and better alternatives from which to choose. Despite the improvements, however, there is still relatively little material compared with that available in other academic areas.

SUMMARY

Written expression is an important academic area for professionals to consider. Though it has received relatively little attention in the past, alternative assessments and remedial materials are now increasing in number and improving in quality. Nonetheless, assessment and remediation of written expression problems necessarily require considerable expertise and time from educators and psychologists due to the number of skills involved and the interrelationships of these skills. Research is needed to further delineate skills critical for success in all five components: mechanics, production, conventions, linguistics, and cognition. This information could be used to focus assessment and remedial efforts more effectively.

2

The Assessment Process

To date, tests have sometimes been used to restrict educational opportunities; many assessment practices have not been in the best interests of students. Those who assess have a tremendous responsibility; assessment results are used to make decisions that directly affect students' lives.

John Salvia and James Ysseldyke (1981, p. xi)

COMPREHENSIVE ASSESSMENT

Given the complex nature of written expression, and the interrelationship of its components, assessment of written expression must be comprehensive. This means that a considerable amount of time is required for assessment. An assessment of written expression needs to consider each of the components of written expression that a student has been taught and that are of concern to the teacher. The assessment should also include an adequate sample of the student's performance for each component so that a sufficient data base is available from which to make decisions. For example, if one were assessing a student's punctuation skills and the test administered required the student to use only two periods, one question mark, and two colons, this would result in an inadequate sample of performance. It would be impossible to draw conclusions about the student's skill level or to develop an adequate data base from which to make decisions about the student's instructional needs. Many tests of written expression do not adequately sample all skills. Hence, examiners need to be aware of the limitations of each test and, when necessary, be able to supplement test results with information gathered informally.

It is also important to avoid overtesting. Because of the number of components involved in written expression, it is easy to overtest in this area. Overtesting, however, not only wastes valuable time, but it also

4

can result in fatigue for the student and examiner, causing unnecessary errors and invalid test results. Usually, overtesting can be avoided by obtaining sufficient background information about the student prior to direct testing.

SOURCES OF ASSESSMENT INFORMATION

There are several sources of information that can and should be utilized in the process of assessment: school records, interviews, direct observation, and direct testing. Each source is valuable and can provide a unique perspective on the student's performance. However, in order to obtain valid information during direct testing, it is important that review of school records, interviews, and direct observation be carried out first, whenever possible. The information obtained from these three sources provides the background necessary for selecting appropriate tests and assessment procedures for individual students. The relationship and purpose of the various information sources is depicted in Figure 2.1.

School Records

School records describe the student's school history, and may indicate whether problems in written expression are a recent development or have been evident in the past. If no problems were noted in the past, it is possible that the present problems are a function of variables in the student's present classroom or home environment, such as the teaching procedures used, a lack of prerequisite skills, or prob-

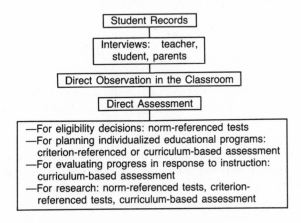

FIGURE 2.1. Sources of assessment information.

lematical peer relationships. If problems were evident in the past, then it may be useful to note any intervention procedures that were tried and their effects. This information could save time in planning remedial programs.

School records may also indicate the presence of medical problems. Such problems may affect performance, for instance, if the student is taking medication. Also, if there are any physical difficulties (such as visual or hearing problems), these may require special consideration during direct assessment.

Interviews

The Teacher

The interview with the teacher is a particularly important source of information when assessing a student's written expression skills. The examiner must determine the skills that have been taught and which skills are of particular concern to the teacher, so that overtesting may be avoided—students can only be expected to know those skills that they have been taught. Hence, when a problem in written expression is suspected, it is not necessary to test skills that have not been covered in the classroom. Further, it is important to identify which particular components of written expression are interfering with adequate classroom performance, since these components will require the most emphasis in testing. Asking the teacher what remedies have been tried, and with what results, will provide useful information for planning remedial programs and help to determine the teacher's willingness to individualize instruction. A checklist for use in interviewing teachers is presented in Figure 2.2.

The Student

The student's perspective on his or her performance in the classroom can also be valuable. One purpose of the interview is to determine how serious the student thinks the problem is. This information may suggest how willing the student is to work on the problem and whether motivation is a factor affecting performance. Also ask the student what is causing the problem. The answer to this question can provide insight regarding the student's response to failure and suggest classroom variables that may be involved, such as not understanding directions or leaving insufficient time to complete assignments.

FIGURE 2.2. Teacher interview checklist for evaluating a student's difficulties in written expression.

1. What are the student's 3 strongest areas? (This could include any area such as social skills, special interests, talents.)

2. Which components of written expression have been taught and about which does the teacher have concerns? Cover the following list with the teacher.

Components of Written Expression	Has been Taught?		Considered a Problem?
Handwriting	manuscript cursive		yes no (If yes, describe.)
Capitalization	yes	no	yes no (If yes, list rules that are a problem:) _____ _____
Punctuation	yes	no	yes no (If yes, list rules that are a problem:) _____ _____
Spelling	yes	no	yes no (If yes, are problems with:) regular words irregular words homonyms
Word usage	yes	no	yes no (If yes, describe.)
Vocabulary	yes	no	yes no (If yes, describe.)
Structure of sentences	yes	no	yes no (If yes, describe.)
Structure of paragraphs	yes	no	yes no (If yes, describe.)

Other concerns regarding written expression skills:

3. Ask teacher to rank order components listed above that were considered problems:
   Concerns teacher most 1. _____
                     next 2. _____
                     next 3. _____

(continued)

FIGURE 2.2. (Continued)

4. For these 3 problems, what interventions has the teacher tried and what was the result?

Intervention	Result
Problem 1._____	_____
Problem 2._____	_____
Problem 3._____	_____

5. Do problems noted occur consistently or only occasionally?

If only occasionally, describe conditions when problems occur and conditions when they do not occur.

6. Ask teacher for samples of student's written expression that demonstrate the problems.

Other comments:

The Parents

An interview with the student's parents may be of some assistance, especially if problems at home seem to be influencing school performance. If parents have indicated difficulties with certain types of homework, this information is important to note.

Direct Observation

Direct observation of the student in the classroom during periods of instruction in written expression is important and also required by PL 94-142 for the assessment of learning disabilities. The observational system developed by Ysseldyke and Christenson (1987), The Instructional Environment Scale (TIES), is a general method of assessing the match between classroom events and the needs of a particular student. With TIES, the examiner first observes the student in the classroom and then uses a structured interview with the teacher and one with the student, both pertaining to the lesson that was observed. The TIES system is learned easily and provides helpful information on variables such as teaching style, curriculum, motivational procedures, and clarity of directions. Problems found in these areas could then become targets for change.

If more specific data are needed, or if it is necessary to measure specific behaviors of a student in the classroom, more detailed and precise procedures for direct observation, such as those described by Alessi and Kaye (1983), would be appropriate. The authors discuss methods designed for school psychologists for collecting data on specific classroom behaviors. Various measurement systems and corresponding data sheets are included. Their system is more difficult to learn, but well worth the effort. A videotape accompanies the Alessi and Kaye materials for practice in using the procedure.

Direct Testing

The fourth source of information is direct testing. Direct testing is not always needed. For example, during direct observation it might be found that the problems a student is having in written expression are due to unclear directions on assignments and inadequate practice on new skills; these problems then become the focus for change. If this remediation is successful, it would not be necessary to assess the student's skills directly.

If direct testing *is* needed, then the tests selected depend on the purpose of the assessment. A discussion of the different purposes of assessment, and the types of interpretation needed for each purpose, follows.

ELIGIBILITY DECISIONS

One purpose of testing is to obtain scores to aid in making decisions regarding students' eligibility for special education services. Test results used for this purpose require a norm-referenced interpretation; that is, the student's test score is compared with the average performance of other students who have similar demographic characteristics (Hammill, 1987).

In order to avoid errors that violate both legal and ethical standards, and that can result in inappropriate placement of students, a careful evaluation of the manuals of norm-referenced tests is essential. There is no excuse for examiners administering tests when they have not read and thoroughly evaluated the manuals.

Tests used to make eligibility decisions must be well standardized. As noted by Hammill (1987), a well-standardized test will have clearly defined instructions for administration, objective criteria for scoring responses, and a standard means of interpreting results. Further, to ensure proper standardization, evidence of adequate reliability and validity is necessary.

As Salvia and Ysseldyke (1981) suggest, examiners must be careful not to abuse the assessment process. Every effort must be made to ensure that the norm group with whom the child is compared is appropriate, that tests are used for the purposes for which they were designed, and that technically adequate measures are selected. Specific criteria for evaluating the adequacy of standardization, reliability, and validity of norm-referenced tests are presented in Appendix A.

In designating a student as learning disabled, evidence is required that a significant discrepancy exists between expected achievement and actual achievement. Cone and Wilson (1981) group the methods for quantifying a discrepancy into four categories: (1) deviation from grade level, including the use of a constant deviation (e.g., 1 year below) or graduated deviation (i.e., deviation increases as grade increases); (2) expectancy formulas, some of which define a specific percentage lag; (3) standard score comparisons, typically using one or more standard errors of difference; and (4) regression analysis. Cone and Wilson provide a detailed analysis of the advantages and disadvantages of each of these procedures and conclude that regression analysis "is superior" based on "critical statistical and measurement concepts," with standard score comparisons a close second. We feel that standard score comparisons are the most useful for written expression because, in regression analysis, it is often necessary to estimate the relationship between the IQ test and the achievement test. Estimation is necessary when using regression analysis because the correlation between the IQ test and the achievement test given to the student is needed. This information is rarely available in test manuals or in published research articles for tests of written expression.

In addition, because of the complexity of written expression, much of the decision making is left to professional judgment, even with regression analysis. For example, PL 94-142 does not state the number of components of written expression that must be significantly discrepant from the IQ results, nor does it state which combination of components would be appropriate. Would a discrepancy between IQ results and handwriting, capitalization, and punctuation be sufficient? Or would discrepancies between IQ results and spelling and word usage be sufficient?

Another issue regarding eligibility decisions has to do with the use of the overall score on a test. Most norm-referenced tests of written expression are made up of several subtests that tap different components of written expression. Scores are generally provided for each subtest, and an overall score is usually provided to describe a student's total achievement in written expression. Use of the overall score in making eligibility decisions has the advantage that the results are based on a larger sample of performance than if only some of the subtest scores were used. Also, because the overall score is based on this larger sample of behavior, it is likely to be a more reliable and valid measure. However, caution is needed in using this score. One disadvantage is that serious problems may exist in several components of written expression hidden in the overall results, which are an "average" of the results on various subtests. If only overall results are employed, some students may be denied services who need them. Another disadvantage works in the opposite direction. The overall score may be significantly different than the IQ results, but this discrepancy may be a function of very poor performance on only one or two subtests. These problem subtests may tap components that one would not want to use as the sole determinant of a student's eligibility for special education services. For example, if a student did very poorly on the subtests for spelling and handwriting, this could result in a low overall score. Yet, if problems existed in only these two areas, it is likely that they could be handled without special education services. Hence, both the overall test score and the scores on the various subtests must be considered in making eligibility decisions.

An additional concern is determining the grade level at which students have been taught enough about written expression so that a valid assessment for eligibility can be carried out. To evaluate for eligibility before grade 3 due to a problem in written expression would seem to be inappropriate. Given the written expression skills typically taught in grades 1 and 2 (i.e., primarily handwriting, spelling, and rudimentary capitalization and punctuation rules), any difficulties could be handled in the regular classroom. Hence, even though it is possible to obtain a norm-referenced score to indicate a discrepancy in written expression prior to grade 3, judgment is needed to decide whether enough skills have been covered in the classroom to warrant special education services.

An advantage of using norm-referenced interpretation of test results is that, if the tests are psychometrically sound, such information satisfies the requirements of PL 94-142 for use in making eligibility decisions. Also, if a test consists of various subtests, results can suggest general areas of strength and difficulty. These areas would then need to be assessed further with tests that provide more detailed information on skill development in order to determine specific skills that need to be taught.

Even if a test is technically adequate, however, there are limitations to the information provided by norm-referenced scores. One limitation is that only very general information is obtained; that is, little specific information is provided regarding skills learned and skills that need to be taught. However, this information is not the purpose of most tests that provide norm-referenced scores. Another limitation is that current tests of written expression do not assess, or do not adequately assess, the more advanced levels of written expression such as the cognitive component. Also, because of the effects of practice, the tests cannot be used repeatedly to evaluate the effectiveness of instructional procedures, and few of these tests have multiple forms.

Because norm-referenced tests are designed to sample many areas, they usually assess only a limited number of skills in each area. Hence, norm-referenced tests are generally not sensitive enough to detect small improvements in skills. Finally, depending on the curriculum used and how the material has been taught, there may be varying degrees of overlap in what is tested and what actually has been taught in the classroom.

PLANNING INSTRUCTIONAL PROGRAMS

Several types of direct assessment can provide the specific information needed to plan an appropriate instructional program for a student. Criterion-referenced assessment is one type of assessment that can be used for this purpose. A criterion-referenced interpretation of test performance results in a description of specific skills for which a student does or does not demonstrate mastery. Tests used for this type of interpretation are based on instructional objectives that make up the academic domain being assessed. The tests can be commercially prepared or prepared by the examiner. Commercial tests typically are developed from a review of the literature and of curricula. A criterion, or present mastery level, is used to evaluate a student's performance of each skill.

Because items are based on material contained in curricula, one advantage of criterion-referenced assessment is that what is tested is likely to correspond to what has been taught. For commercially prepared material, if the curriculum used with the student was one reviewed during item development for a test, then the items are likely to correspond to what was taught. However, the correspondence depends on how closely the teacher followed the curriculum. Skills can only be considered problem areas for a student if the items missed were those that have already been taught. If the classroom curriculum was not reviewed during item development, then the test may not assess what has been covered in the classroom. The examiner must then evaluate the test items to determine whether the test is appropriate for a particular student.

Another advantage of this approach to assessment is that it can include an adequate sample of a student's performance to aid in decision-making, though this is not true of all commercial tests said to provide criterion-referenced information. A well-designed measure will assess each skill at least three times to enhance the reliability of results. Thus, criterion-referenced assessment can provide sufficient information of the specific nature needed for planning instructional programs.

Criterion-referenced assessment does not allow for the norm-referenced interpretation required by PL 94-142, but that is not the purpose of this type of assessment. Another problem with criterion-referenced assessment is that multiple forms of the tests usually do not exist. Because of the effects of practice, these tests cannot be used repeatedly to evaluate the effectiveness of instructional programs. If examiners prepare these measures themselves, it can be quite time-consuming to develop a comprehensive instrument that assesses each skill at least three times and then to prepare multiple forms of the test. A final problem with criterion-referenced assessment is that reliability data are frequently lacking on these measures. However, if skills are each tested three times, this repetition would address the reliability issue. Detailed reviews of current criterion-referenced tests of written expression appear in Appendix B. The reviews include information on the technical adequacy of each test, with emphasis on the skills tapped, the number of times the skills are assessed, and the format employed.

Another type of assessment that can provide detailed information regarding skills a student has learned is curriculum-based assessment. Material for assessment is selected from the curriculum used to teach written expression. This material can be prepared by the examiner or it can be in the form of mastery tests prepared by the publisher of the curriculum (e.g., end-of-the-book tests). Interpretation of results of curriculum-based assessment can be individual-referenced. Interpretation of these results answers some questions about the student such as: Does the student capitalize words at the beginning of sentences? Does the student write complete sentences?

Interpretation of curriculum-based assessment can also be peer-referenced if data are available on the performance of an average group of students. Data on the performance of average peers would provide an appropriate mastery level for assessing individual students (Shapiro, 1987).

An advantage of curriculum-based assessment is that detailed information for planning instructional programs can be obtained on skills a student has learned and those that need to be taught. If multiple forms of a curriculum-based test are available, the different forms can be used for repeated assessment to evaluate effectiveness of instructional procedures. If the curriculum has been sampled sufficiently, results can provide an adequate sample of a student's performance on which to base conclusions regarding the educational needs of a student. An important advantage of curriculum-based assessment is that what is tested corresponds to what is taught.

A disadvantage of curriculum-based assessment is that a norm-referenced interpretation of results for eligibility decisions is not possible because no scores are provided to compare with the performance of a normative group. However, this is not the purpose of such an approach. Another problem is that curriculum-based assessment can be time-consuming, for two reasons: If it is used to monitor the effectiveness of instructional procedures, multiple forms are needed for repeated testing, and these can require a considerable amount of time to prepare. Also, if a peer-referenced interpretation is desired, then data need to be collected on the performance of an average group of peers in the classroom.

Another important limitation is that psychometric data on these tests are often minimal or nonexistent. For example, field testing for clarity of directions and clarity of items should be done. Evidence of reliability of the procedures is also needed. Either test–retest correlations should be available or each skill should be tested at least three times. Ideally, if skills are tested three times, testing should be done on three different days to enhance reliability of results; there can be day-to-day fluctuations in student performance and in environmental variables. Finally, a student may demonstrate problems during curriculum-based assessment because the curriculum used is not appropriate for the student or not well designed—directions may be unclear, the amount of practice on the skills may be insufficient, the amount of structure in the teaching procedures may be insufficient, and/or skills may not be taught in an order that facilitates learning. It may be possible to assess the appropriateness of the curriculum, at least to some extent, by the use of interviews and direct observation in the classroom, for example, by using TIES (Ysseldyke & Christenson, 1987) or the Alessi and Kaye (1983) procedure.

When interpreting results of curriculum-based assessment, it is important to remember that the problems noted are not indicative of a student's inability to learn; instead, they reflect the appropriateness of the curriculum and teaching procedures in meeting the student's needs. This last point applies to other types of assessment as well, but it is particularly of concern with curriculum-based assessment because of the narrow focus on a few skills from one curriculum and the scarcity of psychometric data.

EVALUATING PROGRESS

Another reason for assessing students' written expression skills is to determine whether or not they are making adequate progress in their educational program. Such assessment indicates whether or not the particular educational program being employed has been meeting students' needs. It is especially important to evaluate the progress of students who have had difficulty in written expression; in order for them to catch up to their peers, they must progress more quickly through materials than is typical of most students.

So that time is not wasted with inadequate teaching procedures or materials, repeated assessment of skills on a weekly or, in many cases, a daily basis is necessary. The repeated-assessment aspect of evaluating educational progress makes norm-referenced and criterion-referenced assessment relatively useless for this purpose because of the lack of multiple forms. Use of the mastery tests available with various curricula often are not of much help for this purpose either because the psychometric data on these measures are too limited or nonexistent. Further, mastery tests typically do not have a sufficient number of multiple forms for repeated use.

One type of curriculum-based assessment uses performance probes. Such probes have been shown to have very good psychometric properties (Deno, Mirkin, & Chiang, 1982). Performance probes consist of testing students briefly (usually 1–2 minutes) on a limited set of skills being taught in a particular lesson or set of lessons. When used repeatedly, data from these assessment procedures can describe the effect of a program for a student clearly. (The development and use of performance probes for written expression is described in detail in several of the chapters that follow.) As with other types of curriculum-based assessment, results can be individual-referenced (i.e., whether student demonstrates skill or not) or peer-referenced (i.e., compared with data collected on the performance of an average group of peers in the classroom).

The advantages of performance probes are that they can be used repeatedly, are quick to administer, correspond to what is being taught, and can be psychometrically sound. Performance probes do not provide the norm-referenced information needed for eligibility decisions, but they are not designed to do so. Also, unless a large number of probes are used, they do not provide a comprehensive picture of a student's skills in written expression. Other disadvantages of using performance probes include the time required to prepare the probes and, if a peer-reference is desired, to collect data on normal peers. Repeatedly assessing skills could become excessively time-consuming if probes are not used efficiently (Deno, 1985).

RESEARCH

Research is another reason for assessing students' written language skills. Any of the types of assessment discussed might be appropriate for this purpose, depending on the questions a study is intended to answer. For example, if the concern of a study is the eligibility of students for special education services, then norm-referenced assessment would be appropriate. If the study is concerned with the effectiveness of a particular teaching procedure, then performance probes would probably be the most useful approach.

SUMMARY

A considerable amount of time and effort are needed to assess written expression problems comprehensively. The four sources of information for assessment—school records, interviews, direct observation, and direct testing—can provide important and unique information regarding a student's strengths and problem areas. It is helpful to complete the interviews, the review of school records, and the direct observation before beginning direct testing. In fact, once these first three steps are completed, it may be found that direct testing is unnecessary.

If direct testing is needed, the types of measures selected depend on the purpose of assessment. To obtain information needed for eligibility decisions, tests are needed that provide norm-referenced information; to plan individual instructional programs, criterion-referenced assessment, curriculum-referenced assessment, or both can be employed; to evaluate progress in a particular instructional program, performance probes seem to be the most helpful. For research purposes, any of these measures may be appropriate, depending on the purpose of the research.

3

Handwriting

All the so-called prerequisite, readiness skills can probably be developed naturally without any specific instruction as a consequence of learning to write letters, words, and phrases directly. Since we don't believe these readiness skills need to be developed, we prefer a more direct approach to handwriting assessment, one that can be used to identify young students who are likely to become poor writers later in school life and to pinpoint the specific areas of writing readiness in which training is needed.

Donald Hammill (1986) p. 156

IMPORTANCE OF HANDWRITING

Handwriting is a basic component of written expression. If a message is to be communicated effectively, the handwriting must be readable. This is true regardless of the quality of the content. Handwriting that is legible aids communication, while poor handwriting makes the reader's task more difficult and interferes with attention to the content. At its worst, poor handwriting makes communication impossible. Hence, one goal is to make handwriting legible.

A second goal is that handwriting be produced with reasonable speed and relative ease (i.e., fluency). If handwriting is produced so slowly that a student is unable to keep pace with the rest of the class or requires extra time to complete assignments, this will impede learning. If handwriting is so labored that it results in fatigue, frustration, and even avoidance, then handwriting skills are not functional. When there are problems with fluency, both the mechanical and production components of written expression will be affected, regardless of mastery of other components. Hence, both legibility and fluency are useful to consider in assessment.

ISSUES IN ASSESSMENT

Whether the goals of handwriting—legibility and fluency—are met depends on how well students learn the various subskills involved. Consideration of each of these subskills during an assessment is helpful in planning remediation programs. However, it is not necessary to evaluate these subskills for students whose handwriting is legible and fluent.

Three related and rather obvious subskills that may be partially responsible for problems with legibility, rate, and ease of production are (1) pencil grasp, (2) paper position, and (3) posture. Appropriate pencil grip is an easy three-finger grip approximately 1 inch from the tip of the pencil. In order to achieve this grip, some children may need aids such as pencil grippers or wire frames during the initial stages of learning. Young children may try to use a fisted grasp on the pencil; however, a student who uses such a grasp will have little control. An appropriate paper position is parallel with the desk for manuscript and at about a 60° angle from the vertical for cursive writing—toward the left for right-handed students and toward the right for left-handed students. A comfortable and functional writing posture is facilitated by a desk and chair of appropriate size for the student. Students should sit in an upright position when writing. Left-handed students should avoid hooking their writing hand while writing. Hooking causes unnecessary tension and fatigue for the student and smudges the handwriting.

Consideration of the following subskills helps to isolate error patterns: (1) forming letters correctly; (2) properly spacing letters and words; (3) using a consistent slant; (4) producing letters of appropriate size; and (5) aligning handwriting properly on the page.

Letter formation has been found to be responsible for most errors in handwriting (Newland, 1932; Weiner, 1980a). The formation error noted most frequently in cursive writing is the failure to close letters correctly (Hall, 1981). For example, the letter "a" might be formed to look like "ci" or "u." Other frequent errors include looping nonloop strokes (e.g., making an "i" look like an "e"), use of straight-up rather than rounded strokes (e.g., "m" written to look like a "w"), failure to cross "t"s, and problems forming "r"s and "s"s (Hammill, 1986; Newland, 1932). Isolating the specific letters a student has difficulty forming is necessary in order to determine which letters require additional practice.

If the amount of space between letters or between words is too great or not enough, handwriting can become illegible. Also, if words and letters are jammed together at margins, reading can be difficult.

A relative uniformity of spacing is needed, though criteria for appropriate spacing are subjective (Larsen, 1987). Hammill and Larsen (1983) suggest that spaces between words should be somewhat larger than one lower-case letter. Spacing is less of a problem with cursive writing than it is with manuscript writing because there are no spaces between letters in words and it is more obvious that words are complete units.

Inconsistent slant (e.g., some letters leaning forward, some backward, and others straight up) can make handwriting illegible. Use of a fairly consistent slant contributes to more readability.

Inconsistent letter size can also be problematic. In most handwriting systems (D'Nealian approach excluded; see Chapter 9), "i," "u," and "e" are one fourth of a line space in height; "d," "t," and "p" are one half of a space in height; the capitals and "l," "h," "d," and "b" are three fourths of a space in height; and lower loops of letters should be about half a space below the line (Hammill & Larsen, 1983).

When words run above and below the lines (i.e., alignment problems), handwriting is messy. If the problem is severe (e.g., lines of written material overlap), the handwriting may be illegible.

These subskills are most comprehensively assessed by criterion-referenced tests or curriculum-based assessment procedures. Norm-referenced tests only sample these subskills, though they can provide scores to describe overall handwriting performance.

In addition to the subskills of handwriting other issues also need consideration in assessment. For instance, the form of handwriting assessed should be the form the student uses in the classroom. Further, the skills assessed should be those that are directly relevant to handwriting, rather than those used in copying triangles or wavy lines.

Deno and Mirkin (1977) and Starlin (1982) suggest that material used for the assessment of handwriting be based on reading material the child has mastered so as not to make the material unnecessarily difficult to write. However, this may be difficult to do with young children or poor readers. Deno and Mirkin (1977) suggest that students copy the alphabet in serial or random order. However, copying the alphabet in random order is no easier than copying words a student cannot read. In addition, copying letters does not allow for the assessment of a student's ability to space words appropriately. Also, writing sentence-length material can provide a context that may assist the student in recognizing words he or she has difficulty reading. Hence, for the young student or poor reader, the best alternative appears to be to use material written at a very easy reading level and to ask the student to read the material aloud before writing it. This allows the examiner to correct errors in reading and to prompt unknown words.

It is helpful to note whether the student makes frequent erasures or writeovers (i.e., marks letters over other letters), since these can result in a messy paper that is difficult to read. Repeated erasures and writeovers also suggest that a student is uncertain of the formation of some letters.

It is also useful to note whether a student demonstrates a pattern of incorrectly mixing upper-case and lower-case letters within a word. Weiner (1980b) suggests that this error pattern probably indicates that the student does not remember the correct formation of the lower-case letter.

If a student is asked to copy material, legibility and fluency may be affected by whether the work is near-point copying (e.g., from material on their desk) or far-point copying (e.g., from material on the chalkboard). Thus, the ability to copy both from near and far should be considered, since this information could be helpful in planning instruction.

During an assessment, a student should use the standard writing materials employed in most classrooms. Shapiro (1987, p. 120) notes that "the use of larger ruled paper, larger letters, and larger pencils does not make sense. Why give the smallest hands the largest pencils to hold?" Research findings such as those of Evans and Blackburn (1983) support the use of standard materials for students in any grade level. Hence, it is best to use standard materials both in the classroom and during the assessment.

Whether the student is asked to copy material or to write from dictation makes a difference in the skills that are tested. Copying has the advantage of avoiding problems with spelling and memory. Copying also allows assessment of fluency. However, if a student does not remember what particular letters look like, copying will not assess this problem. This ability is most likely to be of concern during the assessment of young children, with whom at least some material should be dictated. However, the examiner must dictate slowly and repeat the words often enough so that memory for the dictated material does not confound the results. Also, the examiner should spell out any words with which the student may have problems. Dictating material that is easy to read will make dictation less of a problem. Dictation alone, however, will not allow assessment of fluency.

Considerable variation in the quality of a student's handwriting can be expected on a day-to-day basis due to the type of assignment (e.g., copying versus creative writing), the instructions given (e.g., "write as quickly as possible" versus "take your time"), and individual factors (e.g., motivation, health, and personal problems) (Graham, 1986). Graham (1986) concluded that "an examiner should not assume that a student's performance on a single writing sample is an accurate reflection of handwriting capability" (p. 65). Several samples of a student's handwriting are needed to obtain a representative sample of skills. Three samples obtained on three different days increase the reliability of results.

NORM-REFERENCED ASSESSMENT

Below-average performance on a norm-referenced test for handwriting alone would not be sufficient for determining eligibility for special education services in the area of written expression. However, norm-referenced information on handwriting may be desirable as support for eligibility decisions. Norm-referenced information might also be useful to determine whether students warrant further assessment.

However, few individually administered, norm-referenced tests provide scores on handwriting. This may be due, in part, to the difficulty in making objective judgments regarding legibility of handwriting; that is, it is hard to establish the reliability of such results. The current version of the Test of Written Language-2 (TOWL-2) (Hammill & Larsen, 1988) does not have a handwriting subtest, but the previous version (Hammill & Larsen, 1983) did. On the 1983 version, the test–retest correlations (collapsed across elementary and secondary grades) were .85 for raw scores and .84 for standard scores. The correlation for the raw scores just met the minimum for acceptable reliability (.85), and the standard score correlation just missed this minimum criterion.

The Basic School Skills Inventory-Diagnostic (Hammill & Leigh, 1983) Writing subtest can be used with children aged 4-0 through 7-5. For students in this age range, the concern is not eligibility in terms of written expression problems; instead, this test would be used to determine whether the problem is serious enough to warrant further assessment. Items in this test were developed based on skills that kindergarten and first-grade teachers thought differentiated children ready for school from those not ready. The skills assessed include whether a child can (1) write from left to right; (2) write his or her first and last names; (3) copy from a card; (4) write letters from dictation; and (5) stay on the line. Some items go beyond handwriting and assess other skills, including spelling and writing sentences. Of the 15 items, eight assess handwriting skills, and six of the first seven are handwriting items. Hence, for younger children, the results primarily describe handwriting skills; for older children, the results describe handwriting ability and spelling, capitalization, punctuation, and copying from a chalkboard. On a whole, this subtest provides some limited and general information on skill development in handwriting and norm-referenced information in the form of standard scores and percentiles.

CRITERION-REFERENCED ASSESSMENT

The Comprehensive Inventory of Basic Skills (Brigance, 1983), which covers skills typically taught in kindergarten to grade 9, has a Writing subtest with four sections that assess handwriting. The first two sections require cursive writing and involve writing the alphabet in sequence from memory, first in lower-case and then in upper-case letters. Assessment is based on whether the examiner thinks the letters are legible. In another section, the student is asked to copy a passage in either cursive or manuscript writing, and the result is evaluated in terms of slant, size, spacing, formation, alignment, and neatness. Each letter of the alphabet appears at least once in the passage. Correct and incorrect examples are given for each of the evaluation criteria. The last section requires completion of a personal data form including 14 items such as the student's name, sex, address, family physician, and signature. Only the correctness of the information given is evaluated. The test does not specify at what grade levels the skills for this section are usually taught.

The Inventory of Basic Skills (Brigance, 1977) has a Handwriting subtest consisting of three sections covering skills usually taught in grades 1 through 6. The first two sections require writing the alphabet from memory in cursive upper-case and lower-case letters. Evaluation is in terms of legibility. The third section requires completion of a personal data form for name, address, age, phone, birthday, school, grade, teacher, room, sex, date, parent, and signature. Scoring is based on the correctness of the information given. Grade levels are provided at which these skills are usually taught.

The Inventory of Early Development (Brigance, 1978) contains a Manuscript Writing subtest that taps skills usually learned by children 5-3 to 7-0. The first section requires that the student print his or her first, middle, and last names, age, phone number, and address. Evaluation is based on whether the information given is correct. Two sections require the student to print the alphabet in lower-case and upper-case letters from memory, and two sections require printing the alphabet, dictated in random order, in upper-case and lower-case letters. The student is also required to write sentences about a topic of interest; this section is not timed, and evaluation for handwriting is done in terms of legibility, length, and spacing. A sample of a student's classroom handwriting, preferably one involving sentences, is evaluated for slant, size, spacing, formation, alignment, neatness, and line quality. Correct and incorrect examples are given for evaluating these aspects of handwriting, and ages are provided when the skills are usually learned.

The Inventory of Essential Skills (Brigance, 1981) designed for high school students, has a Writing subtest with two sections that assess handwriting. The student is asked to write the alphabet in both upper-case and lower-case letters in both manuscript and cursive writing. This is done from memory and is scored for legibility. The second section requires copying a passage in either manuscript or cursive. All letters of the alphabet appear in the passage at least once, except "f," "g," and "x". Handwriting is evaluated in terms of slant, size, spacing, formation, alignment, and neatness. Correct and incorrect examples are given for each of these criteria, and except for manuscript writing, grade levels are given to indicate when the skills are usually taught.

Though most of the Brigance tests provide a good sample of handwriting and consider the various subskills, there are several limitations to using only a Brigance scale in assessment. First, fluency is not assessed. Second, unless the examiner prepares additional passages for the student to copy, only one sample of handwriting from one day is obtained. Finally, the personal data sections are scored for correctness of the information the student writes. Performance should be also evaluated in terms of legibility, in order to obtain information on a student's functional skills.

CURRICULUM-BASED ASSESSMENT

Unfortunately, criterion-referenced tests for handwriting do not provide a sufficient sample of handwriting skills with which to plan remedial programs. To obtain information that is specific enough for this purpose requires a curriculum-based assessment approach.

To assess handwriting skills comprehensively, students need to write material that uses each letter of the alphabet at least once. The words the student is asked to write, however, should be different each time a sample is obtained.

Figure 3.1 is a checklist for assessing manuscript or cursive hand-

FIGURE 3.1. Checklist for assessing handwriting.

Obtain samples of the student's handwriting from three different days. For each sample ask the student to copy one of the sentences that follow and write the alphabet in capital letters once each day. Use a different sentence each day. These three samples are used to evaluate the student's handwriting with the checklist.

Sentences to Copy

The quick fox jumps over the lazy brown dog.
The strong zebra quickly jumped over five white boxes.
Just now a breeze made the six pine twigs fall very quickly.

If both manuscript and cursive handwriting are to be evaluated, then six samples will be needed (i.e., three samples of manuscript and three of cursive). These six samples should be taken on at least three separate days.

Student's Name: _____

Dates: Sample 1 _____   Sample 2 _____   Sample 3 _____

           Manuscript _____   Cursive _____

Writing Behaviors

Paper position appropriate?   yes   no
     (Parallel with desk for manuscript, 60° from vertical for cursive)

Pencil grip appropriate?   yes   no
     (An easy three-finger grasp about one inch from the tip of the pencil)

Posture appropriate?   yes   no
     (Comfortable and functional writing posture e.g., not stooped over or with head on desk)

If left handed, evidence of "hooking?"   yes   no
     (If yes, target as a goal to eliminate this problem during instruction)

Formation of Lower Case Letters
(For problem letters, include an example, or examples if more than one, of formation problems next to the corresponding letter.)

a ___   b ___   c ___   d ___   e ___   f ___   g ___   h ___   i ___   j ___
k ___   l ___   m ___   n ___   o ___   p ___   q ___   r ___   s ___   t ___
u ___   v ___   w ___   x ___   y ___   z ___

Scoring Formation Errors:
     If a formation problem occurs 2 or 3 times for a letter, instruction on this letter is needed. If a formation problem occurs only once for a letter, additional practice with feedback is needed. If no formation problems are noted for a letter, consider this letter mastered.

Formation of Capital Letters

A ___   B ___   C ___   D ___   E ___   F ___   G ___   H ___   I ___   J ___
K ___   L ___   M ___   N ___   O ___   P ___   Q ___   R ___   S ___   T ___
U ___   V ___   W ___   X ___   Y ___   Z ___

See Scoring Formation Errors for lower case letters for teaching implications for capital letters.

List any letters which are reversed (e.g., b, d,) or inverted (e.g., n, u):

Size of Writing
(If size is a problem for only some letters, indicate this under the Formation of Letters sections.)

Overall handwriting is: ____ too small
____ too large
____ adequate

Spacing
Between letters there is: ____ too much space
____ not enough space (i.e., crowded)
____ adequate space

Between words there is: ____ too much space
____ not enough space
____ adequate space

Words ending at margins are: ____ crowded
____ adequately spaced

Slant
Overall handwriting slant is: ____ inconsistent
____ reasonably consistent

Rate
Handwriting is done: ____ too quickly
____ too slowly
____ at an adequate pace

Alignment
Writing is: ____ sometimes above the lines
____ sometimes below the lines
____ on the lines

Other
There are: ____ writeovers
____ frequent erasures
____ problems with copying near-point material
____ problems with copying far-point material

Notes:

writing. On the checklist are three sentences; in each sentence each of the letters of the alphabet appears at least once. Asking a student to write one of these sentences on each of three different days would provide an adequate sample of this aspect of handwriting. Any letter written correctly on all three samples should be considered mastered; letters correct two times would require additional practice; and letters written correctly once or not at all require further instruction. In this evaluation, upper-case letters are written in isolation once for each of the three samples obtained with the checklist.

Acceptability of formation is determined on a subjective basis, in terms of whether the examiner is able to decipher a letter easily. To assess the accuracy of judgments on letter formations, it is helpful to have another person also judge handwriting periodically by use of the checklist and then determine interrater agreement. This can be done using the formula, [agreements/(agreements + disagreements)] × 100. Each letter (both lower-case and upper-case) and each item on the checklist should be included in checking interrater reliability; an agreement of 80% or better is satisfactory. Though determining interrater agreement requires some additional time, checking reliability either points out problems or provides assurance that an examiner's judgments are appropriate.

Starlin (1982) and Deno and Mirkin (1977) have developed systems for assessing handwriting using repeated performance probes to assess progress in a curriculum, pinpoint problem areas, or both. These systems assess fluency and legibility. With both systems, manuscript or cursive writing can be used, and students can copy or free-write. With Starlin's system, students are asked to write for 1 minute to provide a sample of writing skills; three 1-minute samples are obtained to enhance reliability. These samples are scored for production in terms of the number of letters correct or incorrect per minute (or the number of strokes correct or incorrect when more basic writing skills are tested). Though Starlin suggests criteria for mastery and instructional levels, Shapiro and Lentz (1986) recommend that data from an average or above-average group of age peers be used to determine appropriate mastery criteria. The small amount of extra time required to test and score performance probes of average peers seems to be well worth the effort. To determine average students' areas of difficulty, they could be asked to write performance probes at varying levels, from creative writing to writing sentences to copying strokes used in making letters.

Though Starlin (1982) describes criteria for scoring letters correct in formation, size, slant, and spacing, Deno and Mirkin (1977) evaluate legibility by whether the examiner can read the material and obtain acceptable interscorer reliability. This latter procedure is less troublesome and probably less time-consuming than testing peers. The formula noted earlier, [agreements/(agreements + disagreements) × 100], can be used for this purpose.

A drawback to these methods of assessment is that the material the student is asked to write may not contain every letter of the alphabet in both upper-case and lower-case forms at least once for each sample obtained. Using either of these methods, and asking the student to simply write the alphabet in lower-case and upper-case form, does not assess spacing of words and may be boring for some students. To obtain the greatest amount of useful information, the examiner must remember to evaluate each sample for each of the handwriting subskills and to note the error patterns mentioned in the checklist in Figure 3.1.

Hence, to obtain comprehensive and detailed information for planning remedial programs in both legibility and fluency, a combination of the procedures appears to be the most useful:

For legibility

- Use the checklist shown in Figure 3.1.
- Have the student use standard pencil and paper.
- Ask the student to copy one of the sentences and write the upper-case alphabet from memory.
- If the student is a beginning or poor reader, ask him or her to read the sentence aloud before writing and correct any errors made in reading.
- Obtain three samples of handwriting on three different days.
- For each sample, ask the student to copy a different sentence.
- Assess interrater reliability, at least periodically.

For fluency

- Use 1-minute performance probes.
- Have the student use standard pencil and paper.
- If possible, ask the student to copy easy-to-read material.
- If the student is a beginning or a poor reader, ask him or her to read material aloud before writing and correct any errors made in reading.
- Obtain three samples of handwriting on three different days.

- Use performance probes with average peers in class and use this information to set the criterion for mastery.
- Determine the average number of letters correct per minute for the student and compare to the criterion for mastery.

Use of the procedures for both legibility and fluency should not take more than 5 minutes a day. If a student is just learning to write and the student's ability to remember the forms of letters is being assessed, some easy-to-read material should also be dictated to the student. Dictation should be slow and repeated as often as necessary, with oral spelling of difficult words.

Handwriting samples obtained during a test may not be representative of the quality of handwriting used in the classroom. It is often assumed that a high correlation exists between a student's performance on contrived measures and the student's overall writing proficiency, but this has yet to be documented (Hammill & Larsen, 1983). Lewis and Lewis (1965) found that first-graders made more errors in manuscript writing on a free-writing task than on a copying task. Samples of a student's classroom handwriting are not sufficient for an assessment because classroom assignments are likely to include use of other skills, such as those involved in creative writing, spelling, and punctuation. Also, depending on the nature and length of the assignment, classroom work may not require use of all of the lower-case and upper-case letters or the use of words or sentences; thus, this work would not adequately sample handwriting abilities. For comprehensive assessment, a contrived format could be employed and compared with samples of classroom work to determine whether any substantial differences exist in the samples produced under the two conditions.

SUMMARY

Norm-referenced information on handwriting may provide useful information for determining whether a student's difficulty warrants more assessment, or it may provide information to support data on other areas of written expression for eligibility decisions. However, few norm-referenced tests have subtests for handwriting, possibly due to the difficulty in obtaining reliable results.

If information is needed to plan remedial programs, then legibility, fluency, and the subskills of handwriting need to be considered. Because criterion-referenced tests employ only a limited sample of handwriting and consider only legibility, assessment for program planning can best be done using curriculum-based assessment procedures.

The checklist presented in Figure 3.1 and the suggestions for it use consider legibility, fluency, and handwriting subskills and employ samples of handwriting from three different days, using peer performance as a criterion for mastery. It is helpful to assess interrater reliability periodically when using the checklist.

Other issues that are important for an assessment are (1) using standard-size writing materials; (2) testing the same form of handwriting used in the classroom; (3) ensuring that students are able to read the material they are asked to write; (4) noting error patterns of writeovers, erasures, and mixing of upper- and lower-case letters; (5) considering the individual student's ability to copy from both near and far; (6) keeping in mind that copying and dictation tap different types of handwriting skills. Even with the use of comprehensive procedures, it is useful to compare assessment samples with handwriting from classroom assignments, since different performances may be obtained from some students under different conditions.

4

Capitalization and Punctuation

Unless he is certain of doing as well, he will probably do best to follow the rules.

William Strunk and E. B. White (1972, p. xi)

IMPORTANCE OF CAPITALIZATION AND PUNCTUATION

Although some rules for capitalization and punctuation are arbitrary and may not enhance the meaning of written material, students must learn these rules well. If the rules are not learned, errors will be made that will distract readers and make the writer appear uneducated (Larsen, 1987). Also, if the rules for capitalization and punctuation that enhance meaning of written material are not mastered, then the purpose of what is written may not be clear.

STUDENTS WITH DIFFICULTIES

Learning capitalization and punctuation conventions is not easy, and problems with these rules occur frequently. For example, studies examining the writing of elementary students, secondary students, and adults have found errors in punctuation at all three levels, indicating that either these skills are difficult to learn or they have not been well taught (Odom, 1964). Errors in punctuation are the most frequent type of error in writing (Greene & Petty, 1975).

Ferris (1971) notes that not only must students learn when to apply the rules, but they must also be able to determine when *not* to use the rules. Likewise, Greene and Petty (1975) suggest that students should be taught to avoid unnecessary capital letters, (e.g., capitalizing words for emphasis).

Problems with these rules are particularly evident in students with serious learning problems. Poplin, Gray, Larsen, Banikowski, and Mehring (1980) compared the performances of learning-disabled (LD) and non-LD students in grades 3 through 8 on the Test of Written Language. At all grade levels studied, significant differences were found between the two groups of students in terms of their capitalization and punctuation skills. Problems with the rules were extensive for LD students.

ISSUES IN ASSESSMENT

Most authors agree on which rules of capitalization are important, but there is less agreement on which punctuation rules must be taught. Also, there are more rules involved in punctuation than there are in capitalization.

Greene and Petty (1975) developed a list of capitalization rules based on research that examined both spontaneous and assigned student writing (Table 4.1). The relative difficulty of the skills was considered when setting the order of the skills on the list. The authors point out that this list is suggestive and "minimal." Greene and Petty (1975) also developed a list of punctuation rules with suggested grade levels (Table 4.2).

When assessing student knowledge of the rules of capitalization and punctuation, it is important to consider whether samples of spontaneous writing should be employed or whether students should be asked to correct written material that has not been capitalized or punctuated (i.e., a contrived format). There are advantages and disadvantages to the use of each procedure.

Use of spontaneously written material has the advantage of representing a student's typical writing skills. However, the disadvantage is that, in a sample of spontaneous writing, a student is unlikely to use all of the capitalization and punctuation rules one would want to assess. Also, those skills that are used in the sample probably will not be used frequently enough (i.e., at least three times) to allow conclusions about mastery.

The advantage of the contrived format is that an examiner can sufficiently sample each skill that needs to be assessed. The disadvantage is that performance on contrived material may not be representative of a student's natural writing performance.

Hence, the use of both types of assessment seems warranted. The contrived format can assess the student's knowledge of rules that have been taught and can provide a sufficient sample of performance so

TABLE 4.1 Capitalization Rules

Grade Rules Taught

Grade 1	First word of a sentence Child's first and last names Name of the teacher, school, town, street The word "I"
Grade 2	Items listed for grade 1 The date First and important words of book titles Proper names used in children's writings Titles of compositions Names of titles (e.g., "Mr.," "Ms.")
Grade 3	Items listed for grades 1 and 2 Months, days, common holidays First word in line of verse First and important words in titles of books, stories, and poems First word of salutation of informal note (e.g., "Dear") First word of closing of informal note (e.g., "Yours")
Grade 4	All items listed for preceding grades Names of cities and states Names of organizations (e.g., "Cub Scouts") "Mother" and "Father," used in place of name Local geographical names
Grade 5	All items listed for preceding grades Names of streets Names of places, persons, countries, oceans, etc. Capitalization used in outlining Titles used with names (e.g., "President Lincoln") Commercial trade names
Grade 6	All items listed for preceding grades Names of the Deity and the Bible First word of quoted sentence Proper adjectives (e.g., for race or for nationality) Abbreviation of proper nouns and titles

From *Developing Language Skills in the Elementary Schools*, 5th edition by Harry Greene and Walter Petty. Boston: Allyn and Bacon, 1975, p. 304–305. Used with permission.

that conclusions about mastery can be drawn. In addition, spontaneously written material indicates how well or how poorly the student applies this knowledge when composing material in school.

Burns (1980) proposes another alternative for assessing capitalization and punctuation skills. He suggests dictating sentences or paragraphs that require application of all of the rules to be assessed.

TABLE 4.2 Punctuation Rules

Grade Rules Taught

Grade 1   Period at end of sentence
Period after number in any list

Grade 2   Items listed for grade 1
Question mark at close of question
Comma after salutation
Comma after closing of note or letter
Comma between day of month and year
Comma between name of city and state

Grade 3   Items listed for grades 1 and 2
Period after abbreviations
Period after an initial
Apostrophe in common contractions
Commas in a list

Grade 4   All items listed for previous grades
Apostrophe to show possession
Hyphen separating parts of word divided at end of a line
Period following a command
Exclamation point after a word or group of words that make an exclamation
Comma setting off an appositive
Colon after salutation of business letter
Quotation marks before and after direct quotation
Comma between explanatory words and quotation
Period after numerals and letters in outlines

Grade 5   All items listed for previous grades
Colon in writing time
Quotation marks for title of article, chapter of book, and title of poem or story
Underlining title of book

Grade 6   All items listed for previous grades
Comma to set off nouns in direct address
Hyphen in compound numbers
Colon to set off a list
Commas to set off transitional/parenthetical expressions (e.g., yes, no, however)

From *Developing Language skills in the Elementary Schools,* 5th edition by Harry Greene and Walter Petty. Boston: Allyn and Bacon, 1975, p. 303–304. Used with permission.

Usually this approach approximates performance on spontaneously written material.

It is important that the student be able to read presented material easily. If this is not the case, valid test results will not be obtained. A student who is unable to comprehend the material cannot be expected to apply capitalization and punctuation rules appropriately. To circumvent this possible confounding of results, an examiner could ask a student to read aloud any sentences in which there are errors and to explain what each sentence means. It would also be helpful to examiners if authors of standardized tests provided readability estimates for material that assesses capitalization and punctuation skills. Despite the questionable accuracy of readability formulas, an estimate of readability would alert examiners to possible problems. Unfortunately, none of the current measures provides this information.

NORM-REFERENCED ASSESSMENT

Table 4.3 summarizes the current norm-referenced tests that assess capitalization skills. All but the Quick Score Achievement Test (QSAT) and the Test of Written Language-2 (TOWL-2) employ contrived formats where students are asked to correct written material; the QSAT uses dictated material, and the TOWL-2 uses both a dictation format and a sample of spontaneous writing. Besides requiring capitalization skills, the Writing subtest of the QSAT also requires use of punctuation and spelling skills. The Style subtest of the TOWL-2 also requires use of punctuation skills. Only the Diagnostic Achievement Battery (DAB) provides a separate score for capitalization skills. The Woodcock–Johnson Psychoeducational Battery taps spelling, word usage, and punctuation. The most technically adequate and comprehensive assessment of capitalization skills can be obtained by using the TOWL-2, because it uses two formats.

Table 4.4 summarizes the current norm-referenced tests that assess punctuation skills. The DAB, the TOWL-2 and the Woodcock–Johnson utilize a written contrived format; the TOWL-2 also employs a sample of the student's writing; and the QSAT uses dictated material. Only the DAB provides a separate score on punctuation skills. Again, the most technically adequate and comprehensive measure is the TOWL-2. (In-depth reviews of these tests can be found in Appendix A.)

TABLE 4.3 Norm-Referenced Tests for Capitalization

Test	Age or Grade Level	Subtest	No. Rules Tested	No. Items
Diagnostic Achievement Battery (Newcomer & Curtis, 1984)	Ages 6-0 to 14-11	Capitalization	12	40

Quick Score Achievement Test (Hammill, Ammer, Cronin, Mandlebaum, & Quinby, 1987)	Ages 7-0 through 17-11	Writing
		  Form A
		  Form B
			9
			9
				39
				34

Test of Written Language-2 (Hammill & Larsen, 1988)	Ages 7-6 through 17-11	Style
		  Form A
		  Form B
			9
			9
				50
				39

		Contextual Style (A & B)	Depends on number of rules used in student's story	
Woodcock–Johnson Psychoeducational Battery (Woodcock & Johnson, 1977)	Grades 1–12	Proofing and Dictation	5	7

TABLE 4.4 Norm-Referenced Tests for Punctuation

Test	Age or Grade Level	Subtest	No. Rules Tested	No. Items
Diagnostic Achievement Battery (Newcomer & Curtis, 1984)	Ages 6-0 to 14-11	Punctuation	13	30

Quick Score Achievement Test (Hammill et al., 1987)	Ages 7-0 through 17-11	Writing
		  Form A
		  Form B
			17
			16
				49
				44

Test of Written Language-2 (Hammill & Larsen, 1988)	Ages 7-6 through 17-11	Style
		  Form A
		  Form B
			17
			14
				52
				47

		Contextual Style (A & B)	Depends on number of rules used in student's story	
Woodcock–Johnson Psychoeducational Battery (Woodcock & Johnson, 1977)	Grades 1–12	Proofing and Dictation	6	8

CRITERION-REFERENCED ASSESSMENT

Criterion-referenced tests provide specific information regarding which capitalization and punctuation rules have been learned and which require additional work. Because there are so many rules, comprehensive tests must be used. However, as Greene and Petty (1975) suggest, it is important to emphasize as few rules as possible so that students will be motivated to learn; if too many rules are presented at once, students may become overwhelmed.

Criterion-referenced tests for assessing capitalization skills are summarized in Table 4.5. All of the measures utilize a contrived written format. Based on the number of rules assessed and the number of times each skill is tapped, clearly the most comprehensive criterion-referenced measure for capitalization is the Comprehensive Inventory of Basic Skills.

The criterion-referenced tests for assessing punctuation skills are summarized in Table 4.6. All of the measures use a contrived written format. Again, the most comprehensive criterion-referenced measure is the Comprehensive Inventory of Basic Skills. (Detailed reviews of these tests appear in Appendix B.)

TABLE 4.5 Criterion-Referenced Tests for Capitalization

Test	Skills Tested Usually Taught at Grade:	Subtest	Number of Rules Tested	Number of Items
Comprehensive Inventory of Basic Skills (Brigance, 1983)	1–9	Capitalization	24	95*
Inventory of Basic Skills (Brigance, 1977)	1–4	Capitalization	13	30
Inventory of Essential Skills (Brigance, 1981)	1–4	Capitalization	14	68*
Test of Written English (Anderson & Thompson, 1979)	2–6	Capitalization	13[†]	24[†]

*Nearly every rule is tested at least three times.
[†]Plus those rules used in the student's paragraph.

TABLE 4.6 Criterion-Referenced Tests for Punctuation

Test	Skills Tested Usually Taught at Grade:	Subtest	Number of Rules Tested	Number of Items
Comprehensive Inventory of Basic Skills (Brigance, 1983)	1–9	Punctuation	36	101*
Inventory of Basic Skills (Brigance, 1977)	1–4	Punctuation	10	22
Inventory of Essential Skills (Brigance, 1981)	1–3	Punctuation	17	66*
Test of Written English (Anderson & Thompson, 1979)	2–6	Punctuation	14[†]	23[†]

*Nearly every rule is tested at least three times.

[†]Plus those rules used in the student's paragraph.

CURRICULUM-BASED ASSESSMENT

An easy procedure to use to assess progress within a curriculum is the dictating of sentences to students to write (Burns, 1980). These sentences should require the use of the capitalization and punctuation rules that the teacher is interested in testing and that have been covered in the classroom. Each rule of concern should be tested at least three times in order to enhance the reliability of results. Performance on this activity should be similar to students' performance in their day-to-day writing. The dictated material should be material students are able to read easily. Examiners must be careful not to dictate too quickly, and difficult words should be spelled for students. A record can be kept over time to monitor the progress of an individual student or the student's performance can be compared with the average performance on the task for a group of peers who are average achievers (peer-reference).

In addition, a student's daily writing should be monitored periodically for correct use of capitalization and punctuation. The use of capitalization and punctuation in daily writing will be most helpful in terms of instruction (Greene & Petty, 1975). Some of the materials discussed in Chapter 9 can aid in this regard.

SUMMARY

The most technically adequate and comprehensive norm-referenced measure for capitalization and punctuation skills is the TOWL-2. The most comprehensive criterion-referenced measure for determining which rules require additional instruction is the Comprehensive Inventory of Basic Skills. To monitor progress within a curriculum, Burns's suggestion (1980) of dictating material seems most useful for either an individual- or a peer-referenced interpretation of results. Monitoring students' use of rules in daily writing—and giving feedback as needed—is helpful for both assessment and instruction.

It is important to keep the following information in mind when carrying out an assessment of capitalization and punctuation skills: (1) many students have difficulty learning these rules; (2) both spontaneously written and contrived material is needed to obtain a comprehensive picture of a student's ability to apply these rules; (3) students must be able to read written material they are asked to correct if valid results are to be obtained; and (4) while the rules need to be assessed by a comprehensive measure, only a few rules should be taught at any one time; otherwise, it is possible to overwhelm students who have written-expression difficulties.

5

Spelling

For a child of average or high intelligence an inability to spell can be a crippling handicap because it restricts him from expressing his imaginative ideas and showing his knowledge in writing.

Gill Cotterell (1974, p. 51)

IMPORTANCE OF SPELLING

Wallace and Larsen (1978) define spelling as "the ability to arrange properly letters into words that are necessary for effective communication" (p. 363). Spelling "is generally thought to be the skill of identifying a word, either because it is needed in writing or dictated by someone, and then generating the proper sequence of letters needed to produce that word by naming or writing them" (Guerin & Maier, 1983, p. 206). However, Hodges (1982) points out that "spelling is not a low-order psychomotor skill but is a consequence of complex cognitive operations which only now are coming to be more adequately described" (p. 287).

Correct spelling is obviously an important component of written expression, since one generally writes for an audience, and the reader must be able to read the words written by the writer. Hillerich (1985) points out that spelling is not an academic topic, but rather belongs in a class with etiquette. Thus, "[c]orrect spelling, as opposed to phonetic misspelling, is a courtesy to the reader" (Hillerich, 1985, p. 159). Greene and Petty (1975) also stress that correct spelling "represents a reasonable if not necessary courtesy to extend to readers" (p. 398).

STUDENTS WITH DIFFICULTIES

Attempts to ascertain the percentage of students with spelling difficulties have met with little success. However, Hillerich (1985) cites

1980–1981 data from the National Assessment of Educational Progress indicating that, compared with previous assessments of other students, the spelling skills of 9-, 13-, and 17-year-olds were poorer. Anyone who reads students' writings—whether in elementary school or college—knows that poor spellers do exist!

Several studies have investigated the spelling skills of LD students and students with reading disabilities. Poplin, Gray, Larsen, and Bonkowski (1980) found that LD students scored significantly lower on the spelling subtest of the TOWL than their non-LD peers (grades 3–8). Moran (1981) studied the paragraph-writing skills of LD and low-achieving students in grades 7 through 10. (Low-achieving students were those who met one of the following criteria: no special education; earned an F or D in at least one academic class; not mentally impaired, emotionally impaired, or sensory impaired; or fall below the 33rd percentile on at least one subtest of an achievement battery.) Spelling was the only writing feature where significant differences appeared, with low-achieving students performing significantly better than LD students. Deno, Marston, and Mirkin (1982) found significant differences between LD students and students in regular classes (grades 3–6) in their ability to spell words correctly and in the number of letter sequences correct using the TOWL (Hammill & Larsen, 1978).

Studies with reading-disabled students generally find that these students experience difficulty in spelling. Weiner (1980a) found significant differences between reading-disabled and non-reading-disabled students in grades 3 through 7 in spelling skills. Carpenter and Miller (1982) studied differences in the spelling abilities of reading-disabled students in grades 3–6. Spelling abilities were assessed with the Peabody Individual Achievement Test (PIAT) and Test of Written Spelling (TWS). Differences among the groups were found on all spelling tests; groups were not equivalent in their abilities to spell regular words phonetically or nonphonetically or to recognize correctly spelled words. Reading-disabled students scored significantly lower than their peers on all tests but they didn't score significantly lower than younger nondisabled readers. Carpenter (1983) investigated whether spelling error patterns of disabled readers differed from error patterns of younger able readers or of able readers of the same age. Subjects appear to be those studied in the Carpenter and Miller (1982) study. The first 20 words on each subtest of the TWS (predictable and unpredictable words) were analyzed. Differences were found primarily between the disabled readers and older able readers. Disabled readers produced more unrecognizable spellings and did not use phonetic strategies. Bruck (1988) compared the performance of students aged 9–16 diagnosed as dyslexic with nondisabled children at the same reading and spelling levels (mean age, 7-6). The dyslexic students were enrolled in a phonics-based remedial program at an afterschool clinic. Results indicated that both groups used sound–spelling correspondences to spell, but the dyslexic students' misspellings were less phonetic than those of the control students. These two studies suggest the need to teach phonetic skills to students with spelling difficulties.

ISSUES IN ASSESSMENT

Important to both assessment and remediation of spelling is awareness of what knowledge of the English language a student needs in order to spell. Researchers have concluded that, while there is regularity in English spelling, it is not always directly tied to pronunciation; sometimes it is tied to syntax and meaning (Beers & Beers, 1981). "Although English spelling represents sounds to some degree, it more often reflects the structural patterns and underlying meanings of words" (Anderson, 1985, p. 141). Henderson (1985) points out that there are "three tiers of order" that govern English spelling—letter, pattern, and meaning—and "these come into play gradually as a vocabulary is acquired and as words are studied and practiced in writing" (p. 7). Therefore, students have to have a working knowledge of words.

There is a connection between reading and spelling ability. Poor readers "are often poor spellers, but good readers may or may not be poor spellers" (Blair, 1975). Henderson (1985) emphasizes that a student's first major source of information about correctly spelled words is the sight word vocabulary found in beginning reading materials and that the initial processes of reading and spelling are similar; that is, new words are initially scanned by their letter elements. Thus, a student's reading ability is an important consideration when assessing spelling ability.

Johnson and Myklebust (1967) point out that spelling requires "more auditory and visual discrimination, memory, sequentialization, analysis and synthesis, and integration simultaneously than perhaps any other skill" (p. 239). Considering the complexity of the task and the many skills involved, the question can be raised as to whether testing "process" skills should be a part of the assessment of spelling. Research that investigates the relationships among auditory discrimination, visual discrimination, visual memory, auditory memory, and spelling is somewhat limited but has tended to indicate that some of these skills are related to spelling. With the exception of Bannatyne and Wichiarajote (1969) and Naidoo (1972), most studies have found a significant relationship between spelling and auditory discrimination (DeHirsch, Jansky, & Langford, 1966; Moseley, 1974; Nichols, 1949; Russell, 1955; Spache, 1940). Visual discrimination also has been found to bear a relationship to spelling (Chapman & Wedell, 1972; Nichols, 1949; Russell, 1955). The research with memory factors has been inconsistent: Naidoo (1972) found auditory memory significantly related to spelling ability; however, Bannatyne and Wichiarajote (1969) did not. In both studies, auditory memory was measured using memory for digits. Naidoo used the Wechsler Intelligence Scale for Children (WISC), and Bannatyne and Wichiarajote the Illinois Test of Psycholinguistic Ability (ITPA). Visual memory was found by Nichols (1949) and Hirshoren (1969) to be related significantly to spelling, but Bannatyne and Wichiarajote (1969) found only a low, nonsignificant relationship. Nichols assessed memory skills using words as stimuli. Hirshoren, like Bannatyne and Wichiarajote, used the ITPA, which measures visual memory using nonletter stimuli.

Research that compares good and poor spellers on perceptual tasks is sparse. Lesiak, Lesiak, and Kirchheimer (1979) found that five tasks discriminated between good and poor spellers at the third-grade level: Tasks that require visual discrimination and visual memory of words, auditory discrimination, memory, analysis and synthesis, and auditory–visual integration. Tasks requiring the auditory and auditory–visual skills also discriminated between good and poor spellers at the sixth-grade level. Memory for words and sentences did not discriminate between good and poor spellers at either level.

Considering the limited research available, at the present time it seems reasonable that testing these areas probably will not add relevant information to the spelling diagnosis. Even though research has indicated that some perceptual skills are related to spelling, no research is available that indicates how students who lack certain skills should be taught to spell. Therefore, information obtained from tests that measure perceptual skills is not relevant to educational planning for students with spelling difficulties; there is little or no reference to these skills in recent works on spelling.

Recent research (Anderson, 1985; Gentry, 1982; Henderson, 1985) strongly suggests that learning to spell is a developmental process (Gentry, 1982); that is, there is evidence suggesting that, as a student learns to spell, he or she progresses through various stages. This would mean that learning to spell is not simply memorizing words but is a consequence of developing cognitive strategies. Authors label these stages differently; those defined below are similar to these suggested by Gentry (1982):

1. Precommunicative spelling: The child uses symbols from the alphabet to represent words. No knowledge of letter–sound correspondence is demonstrated. Words are random strings of letters that are not readable.

2. Semiphonetic stage: The child uses "invented spellings" that are approximations of an alphabetic orthography. The child has some knowledge of the alphabet and uses some letter–sound correspondence; he or she is aware that letters have sounds and can be used to represent sounds in words. Spellings are abbreviated (e.g., "BRZ" for "birds"), and letter names are used in spelling (e.g., "R" for "are").

3. Phonetic stage: This stage represents "the ingenious and systematic invention of an orthographic system that completely represents the entire sound structure of the word being spelled" (Gentry, 1982, p. 195). Letter–sound correspondence may not conform to conventional English spelling, but words are readable (e.g., "talafon" for "telephone").

4. Transitional stage: At this stage, the speller begins to learn to use conventional alternatives for representing sounds. Instruction in reading and spelling facilitates the move to this stage. Spelling considers not only sounds, but also how words should look (e.g., "eightee" instead of "ate"); the child, however, may use different letters for the same sound.

5. Correct stage: Correct spelling occurs at this stage but can occur at different levels. Gentry (1982) emphasizes that development is gradual and that samples from more than one stage can exist at any one time.

The stages suggested by Henderson (1985) are similar; however, he includes characteristics that coincide with correct versus incorrect spelling:

1. Preliterate (ages 1–7).
2. Letter–name stage (ages 5–9), where most sight words are spelled correctly, and invented spelling is by letter name.
3. Within-word pattern stage (ages 6–12). At this stage, most sight words are spelled correctly, and invented spellings honor short vowels and long vowel markers; the short vowel letter used is usually one with a name similar to the sound.
4. Syllable juncture stage (ages 8–18), at which sight words may or may not be transferred to spelling performance, and invented

    spelling errors occur at juncture (of syllables) and schwa (un-
stressed vowel) position.

5. Derivational constancies stage (ages 10–adult), at which sight
   words may or may not transfer, and invented spellings are with
   words "most frequently misspelled."

    These stages need to be considered when judging a student's spell-
ings, since error analysis should consider the student's current knowledge about words. However, at present, there is no research that
compares these stages of development to patterns of errors found in
students who have not learned to spell well or students who have
problems in spelling. Also, our experience suggests that poor spellers
do not neatly fit into stages. For example, many poor spellers have not
learned to spell most sight words; in addition, invented spellings
generally do not honor short vowels, yet they are not spelled by letter
name. Thus, while these stages may be important for the average
student, they are not useful at the present time for the assessment of
poor spellers. Hillerich (1985) suggests that "the practical implication
of such research is that teachers should be tolerant of the spelling
efforts of young children" (p. 179).

    The most useful spelling assessment concentrates on the task it-
self—how the student spells words. In addition to determining the
level of achievement, which is helpful in deciding whether a student
qualifies as learning disabled in written expression, the examiner
needs to provide answers for the following questions.

Functional Spelling

Does the student have a functional spelling vocabulary? Can he or she
spell a large percentage of words used in daily writing (i.e., high-
frequency words)? The available instruments do not test all the words
that an individual needs to be taught to ensure an adequate lifetime
vocabulary as described by Fitzgerald (1951); to determine if a student could spell approximately 80% of the words used in functional
writing, it would be necessary to test approximately 500 words; at
95% vocabulary, approximately 2,600 words would be tested. To
assess whether a student has a spelling problem, however, it is only
necessary to sample the student's ability to spell high-frequency
words. However, as instructional programs are put in place, the
student would be taught many of the 2,600 words. It would not be
necessary to test all 2,600 words before a remedial program is initiated because instructional programs in spelling should follow a
test–study–test procedure; that is, testing of words to be learned is
ongoing.

When teaching the student to spell, it seems logical and economical to teach words that the student will use in daily life, that is, to teach a functional spelling vocabulary. It also makes sense to test these words. Therefore, words on spelling tests should be largely high-frequency words. Then, if a student obtains a low score on the test, it can be seen that the student lacks a functional spelling vocabulary.

Words on the tests reviewed in this chapter were analyzed using a high-frequency list compiled by Lesiak from *A Basic Life Spelling Vocabulary* (Fitzgerald, 1951). The Fitzgerald list is based on the writing of children and adults. The 2,650 words on the list make up 95% of the words that a person needs to spell in writing throughout a lifetime. Because the list is fairly old, the words were compared with words used by children in grades 2 through 6 collected by Hillerich in the 1960s (Hillerich, 1978). Approximately 94% (2,499) of words on the Fitzgerald list were found on the Hillerich list, indicating that most of the Fitzgerald list words are still used by children; therefore, we feel the list is an appropriate criterion instrument.

Word-Analysis Skills

Can the student apply word-analysis skills in spelling words? Some words are rule-governed; that is, they can be spelled by applying principles of phonetic analysis or structural analysis or both. Most researchers suggest that some type of error analysis be used with rule-governed words so that remediation with that particular element can be carried out; however, not all writers agree. Hillerich (1985) and Henderson (1985) see little value in in-depth analysis of phoneme/grapheme errors with the purpose of specific skill remediation: Hillerich sees little value in teaching phonic generalizations, and Henderson sees the student's level of development as more important, as discussed later.

It is important to determine the student's progress in reading since many of the skills required for spelling are taught in reading. A student would not be able to spell CVC-pattern words without instruction in short vowels. In addition, children often cannot spell words not in their reading vocabularies. This is particularly important for irregular words.

Errors

For what type of words does the student commit consistent errors: rule-governed words, irregular words, homonyms? Nolen (1980) points out that "a child's misspellings are seldom random" (p. 542). Hodges (1982) concurs: "Since children (and adults) make few, if any random spelling errors, observing and analyzing individuals' spelling errors can reveal valuable information about the development of spelling over time, as well as about an individual's own logical scheme for spelling words at a given time" (p. 289). Henderson (1985) feels that the purpose of error analysis is to gather information about each student's "tacit word knowledge," to "develop a sense of how the pupil is thinking about words" (p. 196). Analysis is done at the instructional level, Henderson continues, because "when children attempt to spell words they are uncertain of, their errors should reflect their approximate stage of word knowledge, provided these attempts are made at a level where the pupil is reasonably confident and experienced" (p. 196). Henderson then cites samples of errors, applying them to the stages listed previously.

Diagnosis, according to Henderson, does not yield a specific skill to be taught; instead, it reveals a range of word study needed. For example, if a student is correctly spelling most short vowels and using vowel markers with long vowels, he or she needs to acquire a store of single-syllable words to examine on a pattern-by-meaning basis; that is, the student needs to examine words for their patterns. However, we feel that, at the present time, sufficient, easy-to-use guidelines regarding levels of development for the assessment of spelling are lacking.

Error analysis for rule-governed words is related to whether word-analysis skills are used in spelling. It is easy to characterize error analysis because of the emphasis on rules; error analysis for irregular words generally involves noting whether students omit letters, add letters, confuse letters of similar shapes, omit the middle letters of words, and/or mix up the sequence of letters (Mann, Suiter, & McClung, 1979; Moseley, 1974; Partoll, 1976; Poteet, 1980). Hillerich (1985) sees little value in this type of detailed analysis because it only deals with specific words. Remediation for a student who omits letters would require the educator to tell the student not to omit letters, a rather meaningless statement. Emphasis should be on teaching the student to attend to the entire word. Thus, it seems the only analysis necessary is to determine that a student has difficulty with irregular words as opposed to regular words, or that both types of words are a problem, or that he or she has difficulty with homonyms. This information would then suggest the types of words that should be the focus of instruction.

There are several other features that spelling tests should have. First, because the product in spelling is usually written, the test should measure *written* spelling, particularly because writing a word allows the student to use visual and kinesthetic feedback in checking his or her response. Second, items on the test should require the spelling of *words*—not writing letters, numerals, or random marks.

NORM-REFERENCED ASSESSMENT

Norm-referenced tests must be administered in order to obtain a level of achievement to make an eligibility decision. Eleven norm-referenced tests relevant to spelling were reviewed. Detailed reviews of the tests appear in Appendix A, and 9 of the 11 are summarized in Table 5.1.

The QSAT (Hammill et al., 1987) and the TOWL-2 (Hammill & Larsen, 1988) have unique formats. The QSAT is designed for students ages 7-0 to 17-11. On the Writing subtest, the student is required to write sentences from dictation; thus, spelling in context is tested. There are 22 sentences for each form, with 155 words on Form A and 158 on Form B. Sentences are scored for capitalization, punctuation, or spelling errors. Spelling words were taken from the reading vocabulary list in the *EDL Core Vocabularies in Reading, Mathematics, Science, and Social Studies* (Taylor, Frackenpohl, White, Nieririda, Browning, & Birsner, 1979). Two spelling series were consulted to see if these words were taught in schools. An analysis of the words using the Fitzgerald list indicated that of the different words students are asked to spell, 66% on Form A are high-frequency words and 68% on Form B are high-frequency words. Any error in a sentence makes the sentence incorrect; therefore, the test cannot be used just for spelling.

The TOWL-2 (Hammill & Larsen, 1988) was designed for students ages 7-6 to 17-11. The TOWL-2 assesses spelling skills using two formats—contrived and spontaneous. Spelling in the contrived format is assessed by dictating sentences for the student to write. There are 25 sentences for each form with 165 words on Form A and 186 words on Form B. The same sentences are used to assess capitalization and punctuation skills; however, a separate score is obtained for spelling. According to the manual, the sentences are constructed so that at least one word to be spelled and one stylistic rule to be applied are comparable relative to instructional grade level. "The grade-level words selected to be spelled were taken from the reading vocabulary list in the *EDL Core Vocabularies in Reading, Mathematics, Science, and Social Studies*" (Hammill & Larsen, 1988, p. 61). It is not clear what this means because words are not coded by grade level. All words in a sentence must be correctly spelled to receive a passing score on that item. An analysis of the words in the sentences using the Fitzgerald

TABLE 5.1 Norm-Referenced Spelling Tests Using List Format

Title	Levels	Number of Words	Number and Percent of High-Frequency Words	How Words Are Selected
Basic Achievement Skills Individual Screener (Psychological Corporation, 1983)	Grade 1 to post–high school; six words/grade for grades 1–8	48	28 (58%)	Taken from 1978 Metropolitan Achievement Test, which was developed by selecting words from spelling series
Diagnostic Achievement Battery (DAB) (Newcomer & Curtis, 1984)	6-0 to 14-11	20	9 (45%)	No information
Diagnostic Achievement Test for Adolescents (Newcomer & Bryant, 1986)	12-0 to 18-11	45	1 (2%)	Selected from the *EDL Core Vocabularies in Reading, Mathematics, Science and Social Studies*
Diagnostic Spelling Potential Test (Arena, 1982)	7-0 to adults	Form A, 90 Form B, 90	Form A, 39 (43%) Form B, 42 (47%)	Selected from two spelling scales and various sources

Test	Grade/age	Number of words	Percentage	Source of words
Kaufman Test of Educational Achievement (Kaufman & Kaufman, 1985)	Grades 1–12; ages 6-0 to 18-11	50	27 (54%); includes first 23 words	Selected from two spelling series, two achievement tests, three spelling lists
Peabody Individual Achievement Test (Dunn & Markwardt, 1970)	Grades K–12	70	27 (39%)	Selected from spelling and written language texts, five spelling lists, dictionaries, and magazines
Test of Written Spelling-2 (Larsen & Hammill, 1986)	Grades 1–12	100 50 predictable 50 unpredictable	50 (50%) 22 (44%) 28 (56%)	Selected using five spelling series and the *EDL Core Vocabularies in Reading, Mathematics, Science, and Social Studies*
Wide Range Achievement Test-Revised (Jastak & Wilkinson, 1984)	Grades K–12	Level I 45 Level II 46	30 (67%) 13 (28%)	Not specified
Woodcock-Johnson Psychoeducational Battery (Woodcock & Johnson, 1977)	Grades K–12	35	20 (57%)	Not specified

list indicated that on Form A 58% of the words are high-frequency words; on Form B, 56% are high-frequency words. Spelling is also assessed on the TOWL-2 by analyzing a sample of spontaneous writing. The student's raw score is the number of different words in the story spelled correctly. The TOWL-2 is the only test reviewed that provides a norm-referenced score for spelling in a spontaneous format; however, the test–retest reliability of this particular subtest is below .60, suggesting that it is not very useful as a norm-referenced measure of spelling if used by itself.

With the exception of the PIAT and the Woodcock–Johnson, the tests in Table 5.1 assess a student's ability to write words from dictation. The PIAT uses a multiple-choice format; that is, the student is required to recognize rather than recall words. The PIAT manual provides data that its authors conclude suggest that scores on a multiple-choice format are similar to scores on a dictation format. However, correlations between the two sets of scores ranged from .43 in grade 2 to .81 in grade 6. It is probable that this format would not identify the good reader who cannot spell. Some students can select correctly spelled words but cannot produce the correct spelling. The Woodcock–Johnson contains a Proofing subtest that requires the student to find errors and correct them orally. Seven items require correction of spelling errors; the other 33 spelling items, in the Dictation subtest, are dictated to the student.

The PIAT, Wide Range Achievement Test—Revised (WRAT-R), and Woodcock–Johnson Spelling subtests contain items that do not require the ability to spell words. The PIAT Spelling subtest includes 12 items that measure visual discrimination and the ability to identify letters' names. The WRAT-R Spelling subtest includes a section that requires the student to copy "marks"; copying marks is *not* spelling. The Woodcock–Johnson subtest contains five items that require the student to write letters from dictation.

As noted in Table 5.1, the tests contain a wide range of words per test: 20–100. It is important to remember that an individual student may not be tested on all items because of the use of basals and ceilings; thus, in some cases, scores may be based on a relatively small number of words. Taking this into consideration, and also considering the percentage of high-frequency words, the best measures of spelling are the TWS-2 and the Kaufman Test of Educational Achievement (KTEA). Both of these tests sample sufficient numbers of words, with high-frequency words occurring at the lower ranges of the tests; for instance, the first 23 words on the KTEA are high-frequency words. These tests also meet standards of technical adequacy.

Only one norm-referenced test enables consideration of rule-governed versus non-rule-governed words: the TWS-2. It is divided into predictable words (rule-governed, based on Hanna et al., 1966) and unpredictable words (not conforming to rules); unfortunately, the authors do not key the predictable words to rules that the student should be utilizing. However, a general judgment can be made as to whether a student is able to go from sound to symbol (i.e., use phonetic analysis skills) to spell words; it is also possible to reach some general conclusions about the student's knowledge of vowel and consonant sounds. For more information, a detailed analysis would have to be done informally or in combination with a criterion-referenced test such as Spellmaster (Greenbaum, 1987).

The KTEA enables some analysis of words. The record blank is set up to allow analysis of errors with "word parts" (i.e., prefixes, word beginnings, suffixes, and word endings), closed syllable (short) vowels, open syllable (long) and final "e" pattern vowels, vowel digraphs and diphthongs, controlled patterns, consonant clusters and digraphs, and single and double consonants. The examiner can also code "whole-word error types." The amount of analysis that can be done depends on how many words a student spells before reaching the ceiling level. Some students may reach a ceiling level after spelling only a few words.

In summary, the TWS-2 and KTEA are the best norm-referenced tests available for assessing spelling. They are technically adequate, provide measures of high-frequency words with sufficient samples, and allow the examiner to do some error analysis.

CRITERION-REFERENCED ASSESSMENT

Four criterion-referenced spelling tests were reviewed. Detailed reviews of these tests appear in Appendix B.

The Comprehensive Inventory of Basic Skills (Brigance, 1983), designed for use with students in grades K–9, contains a Spelling Grade Placement Test consisting of 10 words each at grade levels 1 through 8. The purpose of this test is to "make a quick assessment of the highest grade level at which the student can spell with at least 60% accuracy for appropriate placement in spelling texts" (p. 176). Words are dictated to students. Words selected for the test appeared at their grade levels in five or more of the eight spelling series reviewed by the author. Using the Fitzgerald list, percentages of high-frequency words are as follows: grades 1 and 2, 100%; grade 3, 80%; grades 4 and 5, 50%; grade 6, 70%; grade 7, 40%; grade 8, 0%. While this test can give some indication that a student has difficulty with high-

frequency words, the samples are too limited for determining placement in a series. Additional subtests assess the ability to spell initial
consonants, two- and three-letter blends, and digraphs; add 36 suffixes to base words; add the same 36 suffixes to words in sentences;
add 15 prefixes to base words; and spell number words, names and
abbreviations for days of the week, and names and abbreviations for
the months of the year. Some of the suffixes tested require the
student to know rules (e.g., change "y" to "i", add "es").

The Inventory of Basic Skills (Brigance, 1977), for students in
elementary grades, contains a Spelling Dictation Grade Placement
Test. The student is required to write from dictation a maximum of
eight sentences, containing a total of 63 words. Fifty-seven of the
words (90%) are high-frequency words. Based on the number of
sentences written correctly (no more than one error per sentence), the
student is assigned a grade level in spelling. Because there is no
justification for the assigned grade levels and no normative data, the
subtest is of little value other than for determining that a student has
difficulty spelling high-frequency words. Additional subtests, however, provide useful information on the student's ability to use phonetic-
analysis and structural-analysis skills. Two subtests require the
student to write initial consonants and initial consonant clusters
(blends and digraphs) from dictated words. These subtests could be
supplemented informally by requiring the student to write vowel
letters heard in dictated words. The Spelling–Suffixes subtest requires the student to add 22 suffixes to printed root words. Some of
these require the use of rules (e.g., change "y" to "i," add "es"). The
Spelling–Prefixes subtest requires the student to add 15 prefixes to
printed words.

The Spelling subtests on the Inventory of Essential Skills (Brigance,
1981), for use with secondary students, are somewhat similar to those
on the Brigance inventories described so far. Spelling assessment
begins with the Grade Level Placement subtest (Forms A and B). Each
form is composed of four words each at grade levels 2 through 8. The
purpose of the subtest "is to provide a quick, gross assessment of a
student's spelling skills at grade level for appropriate placement within spelling texts" (p. iii). Because the test is not norm-referenced,
scores cannot be used to determine the level of achievement. However, 19 of the 28 words (68%) on Form A and 20 of the 28 words (71%)
on Form B appear on a high-frequency word list. Therefore, by
administering the subtest, one can determine whether the student can
spell high-frequency words. However, it is not appropriate to place
students within a specific series based on scores on the subtest because
of the small samples of words and because the words tested were not

taken from spelling series; instead, they are from lists compiled according to frequency or difficulty. The assumption made by the author is that spelling series *teach* these words, which may or may not be true.

Additional subtests on the Inventory of Essential Skills measure other skills important for spelling. Several subtests assess the ability to use phonetic-analysis and structural-analysis skills, such as the ability to write initial consonants and initial clusters (blends and digraphs) heard at the beginning of a dictated word and the ability to write a word with a suffix while viewing the printed root word. Other subtests test the ability to spell words needed for writing checks and receipts (i.e., number words, days of the week, months of the year).

Spellmaster (Greenbaum, 1987) tests a student's ability to spell words divided into three categories on eight diagnostic levels (grade K–10). The categories of words tested include regular words, irregular words, and homonyms. A total of 880 words is available for testing. The lists of regular words contain "dependable generalizations" that apply to the bulk of English-language spelling. Words are organized according to phonic and structural elements. Each level of testing has words made up of phonic elements tested on earlier levels as well as new elements. Phonic elements tested include single consonants, consonant blends and digraphs, long and short vowels, vowel digraphs and diphthongs, schwa, vowels with "r" and "l" control, and the CVCE rule. Structural elements tested include prefixes and suffixes. Rules tested include dropping "e" before "ing" or "y," doubling the final consonant in monosyllabic and polysyllabic words, changing "y" to "i." The phonic and structural elements and rules tested are printed on the scoring forms for ease in error analysis. The elements tested appear to be those most useful in spelling (Blake & Emans, 1970).

The irregular word lists are used to evaluate spelling of non-rule-governed words. The first five lists have a large percentage of high-frequency words (161 of 180; 89%). The remaining three contain few high-frequency words (20 of 120; 17%). According to the author, the homophone lists are composed of words "used frequently in speaking and . . . needed for written work." An analysis of the words indicated that the first four lists contain 72% high-frequency words (101 of 140), while Lists 5, 6, 7 and 8 contain only 28% high-frequency words (44 of 160). Thus, for both of these categories of words, the lists at the easier levels are more useful in determining whether a student has difficulty with high-frequency words.

By combining sections of the Brigance Inventories and of Spellmaster, the examiner can gather information essential to appropriate educational planning. These tests provide answers about the student's use of word-analysis skills in spelling and whether the student has a functional spelling vocabulary.

CURRICULUM-BASED ASSESSMENT

Curriculum-based assessment can be used for three purposes (Guerin & Maier, 1983): (1) to place a student in an appropriate spelling book or set of materials; (2) to analyze a spelling problem in order to plan remedial instruction; and (3) to measure progress in spelling.

Placing Students in Instructional Programs

Spelling can be taught using a published graded spelling program, by devising words for instruction from high-frequency words lists or reading programs, and/or by teaching students words misspelled in their writing. Guerin and Maier (1983) and Henderson (1985) point out that, in most schools, all students in each grade are assigned the same grade-level spelling book. While for many students learning the prescribed words each week is not difficult, for others the task is frustrating. Some students may learn the words for the week but quickly forget them. Proper placement in a series, if that is the method selected for teaching spelling, is essential if the student is to acquire a spelling vocabulary that he or she will use.

Henderson (1985) suggests drawing a random sample of words from a graded spelling program—20 words for grades 1 and 2, and 25 words for the other levels. Two or three samples should be taken so that several forms are available. The lists are administered to students sequentially. Henderson (1985) suggests that lists then be scored using the following criteria taken from Emmett Betts (1957): independent level, 90% correct or better; instructional level, 75%; frustration level, 50%. Research cited by Henderson (Schlagel, 1982) supports these levels. Schlagel found that students who miss approximately 50% of words on a test make errors that are not even close to the word. A few students taught at this level may manage to remember words for a weekly test, but they soon forget them. When students miss approximately 75% of words, errors tend to be close to those that "typically occur developmentally" (Henderson, 1985, p. 193). With sufficient practice, students can learn and remember words at this level. Errors at the 90% level are frequently due to carelessness or a "slip of the hand" and "can usually be corrected without extended study" (Henderson, 1985, p. 193). Henderson suggests that if an instructional level is not clearly established and the student is reading below grade level, the student should be placed in a spelling series commensurate with his or her reading level. Once a student is placed in a program, pretests given before weekly study should be monitored closely. Hillerich (1985) suggests that the student who misses more than 50% of words on the pretests should be placed in a lower level.

If spelling is taught using high-frequency word lists or graded lists such as those developed by Hillerich (1985), samples of those words can be selected for assessment. The graded lists by Hillerich are highly recommended for instructional purposes (see Chapter 9) because of their research base. Hillerich includes placement tests for the lists, making assessment much easier. In addition to the samples from graded or high-frequency lists, we recommend that the 100 most frequently used words be tested (Hillerich, 1978). These words account for 60% of all words used by elementary school children (Table 5.2). Ninety-eight of the words occur on the Fry Instant Word List (Fry, 1980), so most students will have encountered them in reading.

Some authors suggest selecting words from the reading program and from other lessons for spelling instruction, because these are words students are required to write (Guerin & Maier, 1983; Shapiro, 1987). Shapiro (1987) recommends randomly selecting lists of 10–15 words from the beginning, middle, and end of each level of the basal reading series. Assessment would begin with the student's reading-instruction level and proceed forward or backward. No criterion for passing at each level is cited.

Whether spelling is taught using graded texts, graded lists, or words from reading instruction, it is important to determine what words students frequently misspell in their writing. The student's writing can be used as an indication of progress, as noted later, or as a source of words that should be taught to the student. One drawback, of course, is that many students do not write words they cannot spell.

Analyzing the Spelling Problem

As indicated earlier, how much and what type of analysis should be done is a matter of opinion. We feel students' errors should be studied primarily to determine whether they have difficulty with rule-governed or non–rule-governed words or both. This analysis may suggest reteaching of a sound–symbol pattern or the need for more exposure to a word. In addition to analyzing errors made on placement tests, analyzing errors should take place on weekly tests. Rowell (1975) points out that most teachers do not check students'

TABLE 5.2 The One Hundred Words Most Frequently Used by Children in Their Writing (in Order of Frequency of Use)

I	there	go	around
and	with	do	see
the	one	about	think
a	be	some	down
to	so	her	over
was	all	him	by
in	said	could	did
it	were	as	mother
of	then	get	our
my	like	got	don't
he	went	came	school
is	them	time	little
you	she	back	into
that	out	will	who
we	at	can	after
when	are	people	no
they	just	from	am
on	because	saw	well
would	what	now	two
me	if	or	put
for	day	know	man
but	his	your	didn't
have	this	home	us
up	not	house	things
had	very	an	too

The first five words account for 18.2% of words used by students in grades 2–6; the full hundred accounts for 60%.

From Hillerich, R. (1978) *A Writing Vocabulary of Elementary Children.* Courtesy of Charles C. Thomas, Publisher, Springfield, Illinois.

weekly tests to determine what words have not been learned; rather, they simply record the grades. Rowell suggests that each student keep a list of words missed on the final weekly test; on this list, the student would write the misspelled word with the correct spelling in parentheses. Rowell suggests that this may be a sufficient step for learning correct spelling.

Measuring Progress

Progress in spelling is easily measured in two ways: (1) performance on weekly spelling tests and (2) performance in writing assignments (Shapiro, 1987; Shapiro & Lentz, 1986). In addition, teachers can incorporate words from the spelling curriculum into paragraphs dictated to the student (Shapiro & Lentz, 1986). Hillerich (1985) views checking written assignments as important for determining whether the student is developing a "spelling conscience." He cites research indicating that students can correctly spell approximately 50%–60% of words previously misspelled in writing when these words are tested individually. Hillerich feels that this points to the need to develop a "spelling conscience," the view that correct spelling is a courtesy to the reader.

The methods noted above use the criterion of correctly spelling entire words. Several writers (Deno, Mirkin, & Wesson, 1983; Shapiro, 1987; Starlin, 1982) point out that counting correct letters is a more sensitive index of improvement. For example, spelling "barometer" as "baremeter" after instruction (eight letters correct, one incorrect) is better than "barromeeter" (five letters correct, five incorrect) before instruction.

Guerin and Maier (1983) suggest a method that makes progress obvious to the student. Words for study are listed on a page in a word column. Other columns are titled "Recognition" (two dates on which the student could recognize word), "Recall" (three dates on which the student met the criterion of writing the word from dictation), and "Use in Writing" (three dates on which the student met the criterion of using the word in his or her writing). Finally, a sticker is placed in the "It's Mine" column, indicating that the student "owns" the word. Pages filled with stickers provide evidence of progress toward developing a functional spelling vocabulary.

SUMMARY

Tests selected for the assessment of spelling should enable the examiner to determine (1) if a student can spell a large percentage of words used in day-to-day writing (functional or high-frequency words); (2) whether the student can apply word-analysis skills in spelling words; and (3) what type of consistent errors the student commits. The best norm-referenced tests reviewed are the Test of Written Spelling-2 and the Kaufman Test of Educational Achievement. The Brigance Inventories and Spellmaster are criterion-referenced tests that can be helpful in gathering information for appropriate educational planning. In addition to the tests, curriculum-based assessment is essential for selecting materials for remediation, analyzing errors, and measuring progress in spelling.

6

Vocabulary and Word Usage

Writing good standard English is no cinch, and before you have managed it you will have encountered enough rough country to satisfy even the most adventurous spirit.

William Strunk and E. B. White (1972, p. 77)

IMPORTANCE OF VOCABULARY AND WORD USAGE

The importance of a well-developed vocabulary is clear. As noted by Greene and Petty (1975):

> A major teaching concern at all grade levels is that of helping children to acquire and use vocabularies of sufficient breadth and depth to make their receptive and expressive language as effective as it should be in terms of their maturity and intellectual levels. Too many adults are able to use only a limited vocabulary, with the result that their expression is colorless, often boring, and sometimes not clearly understandable. (p. 381)

Besides aiding in communication and making written material more interesting to read, vocabulary reflects the writer's skill level. Straw (1981) suggests that, "Perhaps the most obvious index of writing performance is a writer's knowledge and use of vocabulary" (p. 184).

The importance of word usage is more controversial and complicated than the importance of vocabulary. First, various authors define the term "word usage" differently. Hillerich (1985, p. 118) suggests that, "grammar has to do with the way words are strung together," but to the public, "grammar" is considered "word usage"; in many classrooms, "grammar" is considered to be only the parts of speech. In this chapter, the term "word usage" is used broadly as the

58

ability to use the parts of speech according to standard English. However, even what constitutes standard English is open to debate: "Standard English simply becomes impossible to define in absolute terms," according to Greene and Petty (1975, p. 32). This situation exists because many factors affect standard usage: differences in dialect; the purpose of what is written; the audience; and changes in the language itself. In addition, a great deal of research has shown that the teaching of the rules of grammar has not resulted in improved written expression skills. During assessment, isolating rules of grammar that students do not know is only useful if the teaching that follows focuses on these problems as they are evident in daily writing. That is, grammar is best taught when a student's writing shows a need, rather than having students memorize rules and complete drills and exercises focusing on terminology (Kean, 1981). The assessment of word usage in this chapter is approached from this perspective.

STUDENTS WITH DIFFICULTIES

Morris and Crump (1982) found that LD students, 9–15 years of age, use a smaller variety of words in writing than their non-LD peers. Poplin et al. (1980) did not find differences in vocabulary between LD and non-LD students in the elementary grades, but they did find that LD students scored lower on vocabulary use at grades 7 and 8. The different findings in these studies may be a function of different methods of assessing vocabulary use; however, it is clear that LD students tend not to perform as well on measures of vocabulary as their non-LD peers. The age at which this difference first appears remains to be established.

Poplin et al. (1980) also found significant differences between LD and non-LD students in grades 3 through 8 on the Word Usage subtest of the Test of Written Language. Thus, word usage is an area in which the performance of LD students quite frequently is discrepant from that of normal achievers.

ISSUES IN ASSESSMENT

Vocabulary

An important and unresolved issue is how best to measure vocabulary. Several procedures have been tried with mixed results.

One approach often used in research is the type/token ratio. This ratio is the number of different words used in a written sample compared with the total number of words used in that sample. Use of this ratio assumes that a more diverse vocabulary is a more mature vocabulary. Several more complicated variations of the type/token ratio have also been used. This approach is typically used with a computer because of the time required for this type of analysis. Though numerous studies have been carried out using this ratio, or a variation of it, "no solid and convincing evidence seems to be available to justify type/token ratio as a reliable measure of vocabulary maturity" (Straw, 1981, p. 186). Further, Morris and Crump (1982) note that, while the type/token ratio may be useful for research purposes, it has limited use for teachers.

Another approach to measuring vocabulary has been to examine word length. Page (1968) reports a correlation of .51 between word length (in letters) and quality of writing and a correlation of .53 between standard deviation of word length and quality of writing. Deno, Marston, and Mirkin (1982) report correlations between word length and various measures of written expression. Word length correlated .60 with overall performance on the TOWL, .53 on the Stanford Word Usage subtest, and .47 with Developmental Sentence Scoring. Hence, word length appears to have some merit as a measure of level of vocabulary used in writing.

However, in the Deno, Marston, and Mirkin (1982) study, the use of mature words as a measure of vocabulary development was found to have even higher correlations with three measures of written expression used in the study. The mature-words approach to assessing vocabulary development involves word-frequency counts. The assumption with this approach is that less mature writers tend to use common words, while mature writers will employ words that appear less frequently in print. Based on a computer analysis of 101 writing samples of fourth, eighth, and 11th graders, Finn (1977) prepared a list of words that he referred to as "undistinguished word choices." If a sample of writing contained a large proportion of the words on this list, it probably had been written by a less mature writer. Deno, Marston, and Mirkin (1982) used this list to examine the frequency of use of mature words by LD students and their non-LD peers in grades 3 through 6. They found that LD students used significantly fewer mature words. Further, Deno, Marston, and Mirkin (1982) found the correlations between use of mature words and performance on several measures of written expression to be high. Mature word use correlated .74 with overall performance on the TOWL, .72 with the Stanford Word Usage subtest, and .74 with performance on the Developmental Sentence Scoring. Thus, the use of word-frequency counts seems to have some validity as a measure of mature word selection. However, as noted by Straw (1981), a definition of mature word choice has yet to be agreed on by professionals, and the approaches used tend to be time-consuming. (This approach is discussed in more detail below.)

A second issue to consider is that word choice may be affected by the audience, the purpose of the writing, and the topic (Finn, 1977). Hence, several samples of writing may be needed in order to obtain an accurate picture of a student's writing vocabulary skills.

A third issue has to do with the relationship of writing vocabulary, oral vocabulary, and spelling. Hall (1981) notes that if a student scores low on a measure of written vocabulary, it is important to compare this performance with the student's oral vocabulary level. If the oral vocabulary level is higher, then the lower performance on written vocabulary could be due to a spelling problem. In other words, spelling problems may cause a student to limit written vocabulary to only the words he or she feels capable of spelling. On the other hand, if both oral and written vocabulary levels are low, then the focus of remedial work should be on the development of oral vocabulary.

Differences among children in vocabulary use may also be a function of the dialect in the region of the country from which the children come (Greene & Petty, 1975). Vocabulary development is certainly a result of a student's experiences or background.

Word Usage

Differences in grammar may reflect dialects related to social and educational backgrounds (Greene & Petty, 1975). Different types of word usage are appropriate for different places and situations, and it is important that professionals recognize that "dialects and colloquialisms are not necessarily substandard" (Greene & Petty, 1975, p. 47). Balanced judgment is needed in selecting elements of word usage for instruction. Gross deviations from acceptable usage and expressions that make the writer appear uneducated require attention. However, issues such as dialect, language changes, and disagreements about standard English are important to keep in mind when deciding what needs to be taught. Greene and Petty (1975, pp. 48 and 49) suggest that the elements selected should represent "the greatest deviation from generally accepted expression" or those that "are the most severe deviations from the standards of the community."

A second issue worth consideration is the relationship of oral to written expression. Falk (1979) describes oral and written language as equivalent methods of expression and states that "what is known about the learning of oral language production (i.e., learning to talk) will have implications for the learning of written language production (i.e., learning to write). Both are instances of language acquisition" (p. 437).

NORM-REFERENCED ASSESSMENT

There are four norm-referenced tests that tap the level of vocabulary students use in writing. It is important to remember that if problems are found in written vocabulary, word usage, or both, assessment of the comparable oral language area also seems warranted.

The Diagnostic Achievement Battery (DAB) (Newcomer & Curtis, 1984) is appropriate for students ages 6-0 to 14-11. On the Written Vocabulary subtest, the student is asked to write a story about three pictures. Maturity of vocabulary is assessed by counting the number of words made up of seven or more letters used in the story. The criterion of seven or more letters was selected based on studies demonstrating that word length is related to quality of writing. Whether seven letters is the appropriate cutoff for defining mature words remains to be demonstrated by research. A DAB subtest, Synonyms, measures oral vocabulary.

The Diagnostic Achievement Test for Adolescents (DATA) (Newcomer & Bryant, 1986) was designed for students aged 12-0 to 18-11. The Writing Composition subtest requires the student to write a story about three pictures. As with the DAB, maturity of vocabulary is assessed by counting the number of words made up of seven or more letters in the story. The Synonyms subtest measures oral vocabulary.

The Test of Adolescent Language-2 (TOAL-2) (Hammill, Brown, Larsen, & Wiederholt, 1987) is designed for ages 12-0 to 18-5. The Writing Vocabulary subtest contains 30 items for which the student is required to read a word and correctly write a sentence using that word. Mistakes in spelling and grammar are not counted as errors, but students must be able to read the words tested. Though scoring is somewhat subjective, examples are given for examiners to practice scoring. An Oral Vocabulary subtest is provided as well.

The Test of Written Language-2 (TOWL-2) (Hammill & Larsen, 1988) is for students 7-6 through 17-11. Two subtests assess written vocabulary. The Vocabulary subtest utilizes a contrived format where the student reads a word and writes a sentence using that word; 30 words are included and students must be able to read the words tested. Misspelled words, mistakes in punctuation, capitalization, and grammar, and nonstandard English are not counted as errors. The second subtest is Contextural Vocabulary, for which scores are based on the number of different words made up of seven or more letters that a student uses in writing a story about a picture.

The most comprehensive and technically adequate of these norm-referenced measures for vocabulary is the TOWL-2. Though not as comprehensive, the DAB and the TOAL-2 are also reasonably adequate technically. It is not clear at this point whether using words of seven letters or more (as on TOWL-2, DATA, and DAB) or requiring a student to use given words in written sentences (as on TOAL-2 and TOWL-2) is the better method of assessing written vocabulary. Further research is needed to determine which procedure provides the more valid assessment.

Two norm-referenced tests tap word usage skills. However, only one of these tests contains a sufficient sample of students' written word usage skills.

The TOWL-2 (Hammill & Larsen, 1988) can be used with students 7-6 through 17-11. The Syntactic Maturity subtest uses a spontaneous writing format where a story written about a picture is scored for the number of words used in sentences that are grammatically correct. Though results may provide useful information regarding the student's ability to use correct grammar in writing, the subtest does not tap knowledge of all grammatical structures; only those forms the student chooses to use are assessed. Though this subtest appears to be scored reliably by different examiners, the stability reliability of this subtest is low (.77).

The Woodcock-Johnson Psychoeducational Battery (Woodcock & Johnson, 1977) is designed for students in grades K through 12. On the Proofing subtest, the student is asked to read items and identify where errors occur. Five of the items tap knowledge of verb tenses and four require a change in verb form. This is too limited a sample of items for such a broad range of grade levels.

Hence, the TOWL-2 Syntactic Maturity subtest provides a better assessment of word usage skills. However, there is currently no measure to assess knowledge of various grammatical rules comprehensively by the use of a contrived format. (Detailed reviews of the technical adequacy of these norm-referenced tests appear in Appendix A.)

CURRICULUM-BASED ASSESSMENT

No criterion-referenced test is available to assess written vocabulary, and it is difficult to determine which vocabulary words, if taught, would enhance students' achievement in written expression. As noted earlier, isolating rules of word usage that students do not know and giving them drills and exercises on these rules is not the most productive way to remediate problems in this area; hence, criterion-referenced tests would not be of much use here. Rather, the emphasis for remediation should be on "errors the students are making or are likely to make, given the kind of writing that they are expected to do" (Kean, 1981, p. 171). Therefore, a curriculum-based approach would be most useful for assessing progress within a curriculum and for designing individualized instructional programs in word usage. However, such an approach to remediation can be effective only if students are given *frequent* opportunities to write.

The procedure that follows can be used to assess both written vocabulary and word usage. If data are collected on an individual student periodically over time, they could be used for an individual-referenced interpretation of results. If data are available on a given task for a group of average peers, then a peer-referenced interpretation would be possible.

This approach begins with the use of a picture or story starter to assist students in writing a story. Each time an assessment is carried out, students are allowed the same amount of time (e.g., 15 minutes) to ensure comparability of results. To assess vocabulary, words that do not appear on Finn's list of Undistinguished Word Choices (Table 6.1) are circled. These circled words (with the exceptions noted below) are considered mature word choices.

Hillerich (1978) has prepared a list of the 100 most frequently used words by students in grades 1 through 6 (see Table 5.2). Comparison of the Hillerich and Finn lists shows that all but 11 of Hillerich's words appear on Finn's list. Therefore, in evaluating writing samples, it may be useful to add these 11 words to Finn's list: "after," "am,' "an," "back," "her," "mother," "saw," "school," "she," "were," and "two." From the group of circled words, the following are eliminated: (1) any words that are imposed by the topic (e.g., if story is about baseball it is likely to contain words such as "foul" and "strike"); (2) proper nouns; (3) slang; and (4) contractions. Though these words may not be used often, they are not considered mature words. Also, if a word appears more than once, it is counted each time it is used. Misspelled words are included in the count but incorrectly used ones are not. Word variants that do not appear on Finn's list are counted; for example, "talking" appears on the list, but "talked" is not on the list and would be considered a mature word choice.

To monitor progress in word usage, the total number of word usage errors can be determined in the story and a record kept of a student's progress over time with different story starters. The total

TABLE 6.1 Undistinguished Word Choices

a	doesn't	house	no	take
able	doing	how	not	talking
about	done	I	now	that
again	don't	if	of	that's
air	down	I'm	off	than
all	drink	important	on	the
also	dumping	in	once	their
and	each	into	one hundred	them
animals	earth	is	open	then
another	either	it	or	there
any	else	its	other	they
anything	enough	job	our	thing
are	even	just	out	things
around	every	keep	over	think
as	everyone	kill	own	this
ask	everything	know	part	time
asked	fair	lake	pay	to
at	famine	lakes	people	too
away	feel	let	person	try
bed	few	like	place	until
be	filter	little	plants	up
because	find	live	problem	us
been	first	living	put	use
before	fish	long	rather	very
being	fishing	look	reason	want
better	food	lot	right	was
big	for	make	river	water
build	form	making	run	way
business	from	man	running	we
but	get	many	said	well
buy	getting	may	same	what
by	give	maybe	save	when
call	go	me	say	where
called	going	mean	see	who
came	good	men	should	why
can	got	might	since	will
children	had	money	so	with
cleaning	happen	months	some	without
clear	happy	more	someone	won't
close	hard	most	something	work
closed	have	much	soon	worked
come	having	must	source	working
could	he	my	start	world
couldn't	health	near	stay	would
day	help	need	still	years
did	him	never	stop	you
didn't	his	new	support	your
do	home	next	swim	

Source: P. J. Finn, Computer-aided description of mature word choices in writing. In Cooper, C. R., & Odell L. (Eds.). *Evaluating Writing.* NCTE No. 16221. Copyright 1977 by the National Council of Teachers of English. Reprinted with permission of the publisher and the author.

number of errors can be compared with the performance of a group of average peers for a peer-referenced interpretation.

For remediation, it is necessary to monitor the daily writing of students, provide them with feedback on word usage, and have them correct their mistakes. To be effective, this monitoring must be done frequently.

Use of various types of story starters may affect performance and make comparisons over time invalid. Therefore, the type of writing required should be kept as similar as possible from assignment to assignment.

SUMMARY

The most valid procedure for assessing vocabulary has yet to be determined by research. However, of the norm-referenced instruments available to assess vocabulary skills, the most technically adequate is the TOWL-2. The DAB and the TOAL-2 can provide useful, but less comprehensive, results.

For word usage, the most comprehensive measure is the Syntactic Maturity subtest of the TOWL-2. However, this subtest assesses a very limited sample of skills. A more comprehensive measure for word usage would be helpful.

No criterion-referenced tests have been published to assess written vocabulary, and criterion-referenced assessment is not the most useful approach for monitoring progress within a curriculum or planning instructional programs for word usage. The curriculum-based procedure described in this chapter can be helpful for the assessment of both vocabulary and word usage, and results can be used for individual-referenced interpretation, peer-referenced interpretation, or both. The procedure utilizes a combination of the Finn (1977) and Hillerich (1978) lists for assessing mature word choice, and an examination of errors in word usage is also involved. For word usage in particular, monitoring of daily assignments and providing feedback to students are also necessary.

7

Sentence and Paragraph Structure

The problem of organization occurs in the construction of sentences, paragraphs, and extended discourse. No expression—oral or written—is effective unless it is well organized, unless it has been properly composed.

Harry Greene and Walter Petty (1975, p. 367)

IMPORTANCE OF SENTENCE AND PARAGRAPH STRUCTURE

"Sentence structure" is used here to describe various skills needed in sentence construction, although several of the skills to be discussed are classified by some authors as "grammar" skills (e.g., run-on sentences, subject–predicate agreement). Skills addressed include avoidance of run-on sentences, fragments, and verbiage; inclusion of necessary information; use of different types of sentences; subject–verb agreement; placement of modifiers and antecedents; tense agreement; and parallel construction. Many of these skills are also included in definitions of "syntax." However, definitions of "syntax," vary widely, ranging from knowledge of grammar and word order to proficiency in grammar, punctuation, word order, *and* paragraphing. The definition of sentence structure used here may be simplistic in light of the complexity of language and the linguistics component; however, given the lack of agreement on terms such as "grammar" and "syntax," as well as the level of sophistication of current assessment instruments and procedures, this use of terminology appears to be practical.

"Paragraph structure" describes the various skills needed in constructing paragraphs, such as the use of topic sentences and appropriate transition words.

In order for writing to convey the writer's intended meaning, the information must be well organized. Organization must be evident at the different levels of writing: sentences and paragraphs.

STUDENTS WITH DIFFICULTIES

Differences between LD and non-LD students in sentence and paragraph knowledge have been noted in several studies. Moran (1981) observed that plural noun errors and subject–predicate and number-agreement errors occurred frequently in the writing of both LD and low-achieving students in grades 7 through 10. Hall (1981) noted that poor writers tend to rely on simple sentences. Morris and Crump (1982) found that 9–15-year-old non-LD students used more syntactically mature writing than LD students. In examining the expository writing of LD students and their non-LD peers, Thomas, Englert, and Gregg (1987) found that 84% of the syntactical errors made by LD students in grades 6 and 7 were due to the use of a phrase instead of a sentence. Further, they observed that LD students used more redundancies and irrelevant information than their non-LD peers. Weiner (1980a) examined the written expression of reading-disabled boys and their nondisabled peers and found that the reading-disabled boys exhibited major problems with word order, omissions, run-on sentences, and paragraphing skills. Hence, it is clear that sentence and paragraph construction poses serious problems for students with academic difficulties in the language area.

NORM-REFERENCED ASSESSMENT

The Test of Adolescent Language-2, for students aged 12-0 to 18-5, has a subtest titled Written Grammar. This subtest requires that students combine two or more sentences into one comprehensive sentence. Thus, knowledge of sentence construction is assessed, including use of phrases and introductory clauses.

The TOWL-2 (Hammill & Larsen, 1988) has two subtests that assess knowledge of sentence structure, both of which use a contrived format. The Sentence Combining subtest involves up to 25 items requiring a student to combine two or more short sentences into one sentence. In order to accomplish this, the student must be able to write using embedded phrases and adjectives in sequence. The Logical Sentences subtest involves up to 25 sentences that do not make sense. A student must read each sentence, recognize what is illogical in the material, and rewrite the sentence so that it does make sense. In this way, logical thinking in sentence composition is assessed. Reading should not confound results to any great degree as words used are at the third-grade level or below. Though both of these tests provide useful information, the TOWL-2 is more comprehensive.

No tests currently available provide a norm-referenced score to describe knowledge of paragraph construction.

CURRICULUM-BASED ASSESSMENT

How to best measure skills in sentence and paragraph construction is not clear at this time. In an attempt to devise a measure to assess skills in the use of syntax, Hunt (1965) proposed the T-unit or "minimal terminal unit." The T-unit consists of a main clause and connected subordinate clauses (Hunt, 1965, p. 20). A considerable amount of research has been carried out using the T-unit, and findings have shown that the T-unit tends to increase in length as language skills develop (Hunt, 1965; O'Donnell, Griffin, & Norris, 1967). Several alternative procedures incorporating the T-unit and taking other variables into consideration (such as the proportion of different types of sentences and verb expansions) have been developed, such as the Syntactic Density Score (Golub & Frederick, 1971). Though such approaches seem to be valid and to be useful in research, most require computer technology and a considerable amount of time, thus limiting their use in the classroom. Also, many questions regarding their usefulness remain to be answered: What variables determine growth in this area? How can instruction be planned to enhance syntactic development? Straw (1981) points out that, though the measures can provide useful information, they are only "gross indices of growth" (p. 192). He further suggests that, "One of the major problems of research in syntactic development has been that a valid, reliable measure of syntactic maturity has not yet been developed" (p. 192).

Given the questions that remain regarding the reliability of procedures such as the T-unit or Syntactic Density Score, and the time-consuming nature of their application, this chapter focuses on a more skills-oriented approach to assessment of sentence and paragraph construction. Information obtained from the use of the procedures that follow can aid in instructional planning. However, as with word usage, instruction in sentence and paragraph construction should be carried out on a need-to-know basis as problems become evident in students' writing—and this remedial approach can be effective only if students are given frequent opportunities to write.

The checklist that follows can be used to assess knowledge of sentence structure on an informal basis. It includes issues that are important to consider in the assessment of these skills.

Checklist for Assessing Knowledge of Sentence Structure

Greene and Petty (1975) note that the following problems occur frequently in sentences written by elementary school students. However, Hall (1981) points out that run-on sentences are a normal occurrence for first and second graders. She suggests that after grade 4, however, run-on sentences are not developmentally normal. Run-on sentences that appear in the writing of older students are often a result of problems with punctuation skills or of insufficient proof-reading. Hence, it is useful to note whether the student does any of the following:

- Avoids run-on sentences (for students in grade 3 and up) _____
- Avoids fragments   _____
- Avoids too many short, choppy sentences   _____
- Avoids including unnecessary information   _____
- Includes all necessary information   _____

Hall (1981) notes that the use of a variety of sentence patterns increases the effectiveness of written expression. Hence, it should be helpful to note whether the student uses a variety of sentence types:

- Simple sentences   _____
- Compound sentences   _____
- Complex sentences   _____
- Compound-complex sentences   _____

Marzano and DiStefano (1978) found that, though elementary school students make errors in subject–verb agreement, these errors do not occur frequently in their writing because these students employ few intervening phrases (i.e., they tend to use simple sentence structures). Hence, Marzano and DiStefano suggest that professionals not over-emphasize subject–verb agreement and pronoun, antecedent, and tense agreement for elementary students; however, from junior high on, considerable attention should be given to these skills. Hence, for junior high and high school students, one should note whether any of the following appear in the student's writing:

- Subject–verb agreement _____
- Correct placement of modifiers and antecedents _____
- Parallel construction _____
- Consistent verb tense used throughout _____

Checklist for Assessing Paragraph Structure

The following list for constructing paragraphs is based on skills suggested by several authors (Burns, 1980; Greene & Petty, 1975; Poteet, 1979; Starlin, 1982; Wallace, Cohen, & Polloway, 1987). This list should be considered a guide for instructional planning, not a set of standards for students. It is also important to note that skills in paragraph construction usually are not taught before grade 3 (Hammill & Poplin, 1982); hence, the following skills will not usually be evident until after this grade. On the other hand, most of the skills usually have been learned by grade 8 (Hammill & Poplin, 1982).

- Are paragraphs indented about five spaces? _____
- Do the paragraphs each deal with a single topic (i.e., a major idea)? _____
- Are topical sentences used? _____
- Are all sentences related to the topic? _____
- Are the sentences presented in a logical order? _____
- Are the paragraphs presented in a logical order? _____
- If there is a long paragraph, is there a logical conclusion? ____
- Are adequate transitional words, phrases, and/or sentences used? _____

SUMMARY

Problems with sentence and paragraph construction appear frequently with students with learning difficulties. The TOAL-2 and the TOWL-2 provide norm-referenced assessment of some aspects of sentence knowledge, though the TOWL-2 samples skills more extensively. More research on how best to measure these skills would be beneficial. No test provides a norm-referenced score for paragraph knowledge at the present time. Checklists for assessing knowledge of sentence and paragraph construction can aid in focusing on skills needing instruction; however, these skills should be taught on a need-to-know basis with students given frequent opportunities to write.

8

Production and Quality

The process of continually monitoring progress on IEP (in-dividualized educational program) objectives, modifying programs, and evaluating the effects of program modifications may well be the key to developing appropriate educational programs in the least restrictive environment.

Stanley Deno, Douglas Marston, and Phyllis Mirkin (1982, p. 368)

IMPORTANCE OF PRODUCTION AND QUALITY

The number of words students are able to write is an important factor to consider when assessing written expression ability. A sufficient amount of written material needs to be generated in order to transmit a meaningful message clearly; for example, a writer cannot develop an idea fully (i.e., provide supportive and descriptive detail and make relevant generalizations) nor write interesting material with only a few short, choppy sentences.

Deno, Marston, and Mirkin (1982) found high correlations between a measure of production and the overall Written Language Quotient on the TOWL ($r = .65$); between production and the Stanford Word Usage subtest ($r = .62$); and between production and Developmental Sentence Scoring ($r = .84$). Hence, the total number of words written appears to have considerable validity as an overall measure of written expression ability.

"Quality of writing" is the overall impression that a piece of writing makes on a reader. This impression is certainly important if written material is to be perceived as credible and if it is to convey the intended message effectively. However, the construct of "quality of writing" is vague, and judgments of quality usually are based on internal norms. Unless quality of writing is approached systematically in assessment, judgments tend to be highly unreliable (Diedrick, 1974).

STUDENTS WITH DIFFICULTIES

The problem of generating a sufficient amount of written material is evident with LD students. Studies (Deno, Marston, & Mirkin, 1982; Myklebust, 1973; Poteet, 1979) have found that LD students write fewer words than their non-LD peers. Thomas et al. (1987) observed that LD students were five times as likely as their non-LD peers to terminate their writing prematurely. The authors noted that "the problem seemed representative of difficulties in generating multiple ideas related to a topic rather than a problem of syntactical control" (p. 26). In a study by Weiner (1980a), it was found that given the same amount of time to write, nondisabled readers wrote nearly twice as many words as reading-disabled students. Likewise, Hermreck (1979) reported that non-LD students wrote an average of 42% more words per essay than LD students. Hence, total words written appears to discriminate between these two groups of students.

ISSUES IN ASSESSMENT

When planning instruction, it is necessary to assess students' progress in response to instruction frequently. The need for repeated assessment rules out the use of norm- and criterion-referenced tests. Probably because of the time required and the ease of use, progress is typically assessed on the basis of teacher opinion. However, to assess progress using teachers' judgments, rather than a more systematic, reliable, and valid assessment procedure, can be a mistake. For example, Fuchs, Fuchs, and Warren (1982) asked special education teachers how they monitored students' progress toward curriculum goals. The teachers indicated they used their observations for this purpose. The authors compared teachers' judgments of students' achievement of goals with actual student performance. Results indicated a significant difference between teachers' judgments and actual achievement, with teachers judging that more students had achieved the goals than actually had achieved them.

The information that follows on the assessment of production and quality offers alternatives to teacher judgment. The procedures provide overall measures of progress in written expression rather than information regarding mastery of particular skills. To be practical, such procedures must not require a great deal of time; hence, both procedures require only a few minutes to administer and score. It is also possible, and definitely desirable, to periodically assess the interrater reliability of these results.

CURRICULUM-BASED ASSESSMENT

Production

An easy and efficient procedure with which to assess whether students are able to produce a sufficient amount of written material is to use periodic performance probes. The information gained from performance probes can be used to assess progress within a curriculum; probes can also provide supportive evidence that a serious problem does or does not exist in overall written expression if a peer-referenced interpretation is employed.

Deno, Mirkin, and Wesson (1983) describe a procedure for using performance probes where the criterion for adequate performance can be based on the average performance of students within a particular classroom or school district (i.e., local micronorms); alternately, data they obtained from a national sample of over 500 students in grades 1 through 6 can be used. To use performance probes, three story starters (i.e., a phrase or a sentence that provides an interesting idea to begin a story) are administered. Students are given 3 minutes to write each story. For each of the three stories, the total number of words that were written are counted. Misspelled words are included in the total.

Data from the national sample tested by Deno et al. (1983) can be used as criteria for acceptable performance (Table 8.1). To use these data, multiply the middle score from the three stories by the multiplier listed for the student's grade level; this multiplier describes the average rate of progress over 9 months for the students in the sample. The resulting number is then added to the mean score for average students in the appropriate grade in the third column; the total is divided by 2. The result describes the student's current level of performance. The mean score for average students at the student's grade level could be used as the long-term goal for the student.

If desired, the score for average students in a particular local classroom could be used as the criterion for adequate performance. Data from three story starters would have to be obtained for students in the classroom and the mean for the class determined. This type of information could be obtained for a school district as well, with the information provided for each grade level.

TABLE 8.1 Criteria for Acceptable Levels of Production

Grade	Multiplier	Mean Score for Average Students
1	2.6	14.7
2	1.6	27.8
3	1.2	36.6
4	1.1	40.9
5	1.1	49.1
6	1.1	53.3

Source: S. L. Deno, P. K. Mirkin, & C. Wesson, 1983. How to write effective data-based IEPs. *Teaching Exceptional Children, 16,* pp. 99-104. Copyright 1983 by the Council for Exceptional Children. Used with permission of the publisher.

Periodic probes with story starters for 3 minutes of writing could then be used to evaluate the overall progress of students with writing difficulties over the course of instruction. Progress toward the criterion would suggest that the instruction was effective; lack of progress would indicate a need for a change in instruction. If lack of progress is observed, then the criterion-referenced tests, curriculum-based assessment procedures, or informal procedures described in the previous chapters could be used to pinpoint skills that need to be taught.

The strength of performance probes is that they can be used frequently to provide information to compare a student's performance to that of his or her peers as a measure of overall written language ability. Further, the probes require very little time to administer and score. Deno, Marston, and Mirkin (1982) have presented research to suggest the validity of this approach.

As useful and efficient as performance probes can be, further research on their use could be very beneficial. Shapiro and Lentz (1986) point out that clarification is needed regarding the length of the probes, the frequency of their use, and the types that can provide the most reliable and valid information. These authors also suggest that a consistent standard is needed to which to compare students with problems. Though peer-referencing can be useful, the reliability of the procedures used to sample peers could be problematic.

Quality

To define what characteristics contribute to quality of written material is difficult and certainly open to debate. Yet teachers must make judgments regarding the quality of students' writing. No norm-referenced test comprehensively assesses this aspect of written expression. However, the TOWL-2 (Hammill & Larsen, 1988) contains a subtest, Thematic Maturity, that may provide some information that helps describe skills that contribute to writing quality. In this subtest, the story that a student writes in response to a picture is scored for use of skills such as having an ending, a title, use of dialogue or monologue, use of humor, and development of the characters in the story.

One procedure for evaluating the quality of students' written work, holistic evaluation, has received considerable attention. Use of this procedure can make teachers' judgments valid and reliable if the procedure is appropriately employed (Straw, 1981). Holistic evaluation is based on the general impression a writing sample makes on a reader. This judgment is not made on a random basis. Rather, evaluators who use this approach typically are trained to use scoring guides, or previously agreed-on criteria, until they reach acceptable levels of reliability in rating. The rating scales can range from relatively simple (e.g., a 4-point scale of excellent, adequate, deficient, and unacceptable) to relatively complex. Usually, detailed criteria are prepared to describe each level of the scale, and examples may be included. Once a rater is trained, the procedure is efficient to use, usually requiring only 1–2 minutes per paper. A detailed presentation of holistic evaluation can be found in Cooper (1977).

Primary trait scoring is very similar to holistic evaluation, except that students are asked to meet a specific objective on the writing task, for instance, to assume the role of another person or arrange story events in order so that the sequence is obvious. With this approach, the rating scale is designed to fit the particular objective stated. While holistic evaluation provides a very general judgment regarding overall quality, primary trait scoring provides a judgment regarding a student's ability to accomplish a particular objective. A detailed description of this procedure, and the theory behind it, can be found in Lloyd-Jones (1977).

Both holistic evaluation and primary trait scoring can be used repeatedly to monitor student progress in response to instruction. However, specifying the evaluation criteria to be used is essential before scoring. If this is not done, very unreliable results are likely to be obtained. For example, Diedrick (1974) examined interrater agreement for 60 raters on the same set of papers and found a median correlation of only .31; a minimum of .80 should be obtained if reliable judgments are to be made. Diedrich suggested that this low correlation was a function of the raters' attending to different aspects of writing, with some focusing on punctuation and spelling and others on organization and flavor. Hence, it is critical to establish interrater reliability between at least two raters before actual scoring is carried out. Even after sufficient reliability has been established, raters can drift in their judgments, so interrater reliability should be checked periodically.

SUMMARY

Student progress in response to instruction should be assessed frequently to ensure effective instruction. This progress is often assessed on the basis of teacher judgment, which tends to be unreliable. However, efficient procedures for assessment of overall progress in written expression are available that can be used repeatedly and reliably. For instance, performance probes (Deno et al., 1982) can be employed to assess the productivity aspect of written expression. Holistic evaluation and primary trait scoring can be used to evaluate the quality of written expression. Assessment of production, quality, or both can be used to evaluate the effect of instruction on overall written expression.

9

Remediation of Written Expression Problems

One learns to write by writing.
Robert Hillerich (1985, p. vi)

TEACHING WRITING

Hillerich (1985) cites several studies that indicate that little time is spent in schools teaching students to write:

> [Observation of most writing lessons will reveal] teaching such as is seen no where else in the world of education. Most often the lesson consists of (1) assigning or stimulating a topic, (2) having pupils write, (3) possibly admonishing them to proofread their papers, and (4) going error hunting through the papers with a red pencil. In other words, no teaching takes place. (p. 3)

Our work with students with learning problems indicates that the focus of remedial efforts is usually on the separate skills of writing, that is, on completing pages and pages of exercises on the parts of speech or capitalization or completing a spelling book. An entire year may go by with the student writing only one "story" or one "letter." One of the authors recently heard a seventh-grade special-education student explain that he could not possibly write a story because he had not written one in 3 years!

We believe, as Hillerich (1985) believes, "the purpose of writing is to communicate . . . One puts words in print to convey ideas, information, or feelings to a reader. No one writes (except unfortunately, in some school situations) in order to string together correctly spelled words with proper punctuation and capitalization" (p. 6).

We believe that, with the exception of formal instruction in handwriting and spelling, written expression skills should be taught as part of the writing process. In other words, if the student shows a need to learn or practice a punctuation skill, that instruction and practice should be provided.

This chapter is written with these beliefs in mind. The focus is on remediation of handwriting skills, spelling skills, and composition skills (including capitalization, punctuation, vocabulary, word usage, and sentence and paragraph structure).

HANDWRITING

Despite the influence of new technologies, the computer, word processing, and key boarding have not replaced the need to learn how to print or write. K. Koenke (1986, p. 214)

Handwriting is basic to written communication because it is the tool of that communication. Unless the intended message is typed, it must be handwritten. The need to teach legible handwriting to students is obvious. But handwriting is also important after graduation. Throughout life, it is necessary to write on a day-to-day basis, as in writing a note or letter, writing a grocery list, copying a recipe, jotting notes, and filling out an application for a job. Learning to handwrite legibly is imperative. Problems in handwriting can interfere with communication if the writer must stop to think how to form letters or if writing is so slow as to be burdensome. Therefore, all students need to learn to write legibly and fluently in manuscript or cursive to function on a day-to-day basis in school and daily life. There are some students whose lack of fluency requires alternatives to handwriting (e.g., taping lectures or typing work), but there are still many times when handwriting is necessary.

Methods of Handwriting

What method of handwriting should be taught? The two basic forms of handwriting are manuscript and cursive (see Figure 9.1). Manuscript writing can be taught using "ball-stick" or "one-continuous-stroke" methods. One-continuous-stroke writing can be taught with a straight form or on a slant. With students who have great difficulty connecting separate pieces of letters, use of a manuscript form where letters are formed with one continuous stroke or use of cursive writing is recommended. A fairly recent innovation in handwriting systems is D'Nealian handwriting (Thurber, 1978, 1981, 1987), a form of slanted one-stroke manuscript (see Figure 9.2). D'Nealian handwriting, which was designed to ease the transition to cursive writing, has made the choice of manuscript or cursive somewhat of a moot point. However, if a form other than D'Nealian is used with students with severe handwriting problems, it is best to select either manuscript or cursive and help the student to learn that one type of writing well, rather than expecting the student to learn both manuscript and cursive.

Research about Handwriting Instruction

Many of the "current practices in handwriting instruction, . . . are guided by traditional wisdom and commercial materials" (Askov & Peck, 1982, p. 766). However, research, most of which has been done with general education students, is available concerning several aspects of handwriting instruction. These studies are summarized in the following list:

1. Handwriting is not an innate ability. Handwriting skills must be developed (Furner, 1969a, 1969b).
2. Handwriting is a perceptual-motor act. Methods of handwriting instruction "should stress perceptual development [and] should help children to recognize form, to notice likenesses and differences" (Furner, 1969a; see also Askov & Peck,

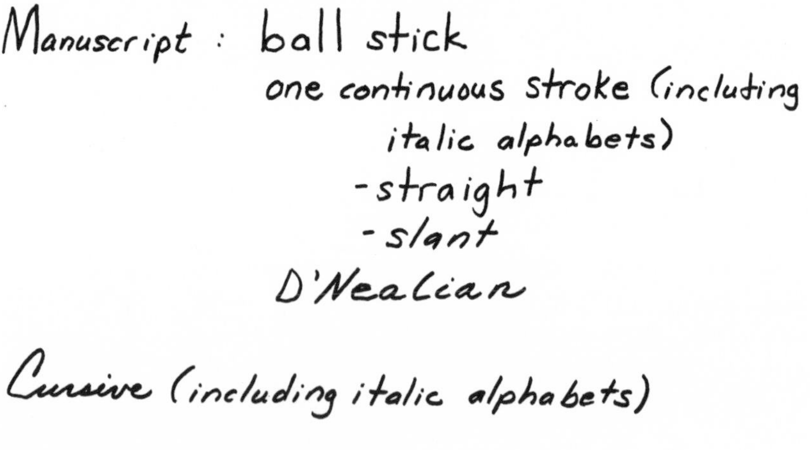

FIGURE 9.1. Forms of handwriting.

1982). Research by Furner (1969b, 1970) supports the use of visual, auditory, and kinesthetic cues in instruction.

3. Research indicates that the handwriting forms taught generally do not make a difference in students' abilities to read typeset letters (Koenke, 1986).

4. Research reviews have lead to the conclusion that "manuscript writing should be retained beyond the primary grades, because it is more legible and more easily learned, and it can be written at least as fast as cursive writing" (Askov & Peck, 1982). We interpret this finding to mean that instruction in cursive writing is not essential.

5. Research does not support the superiority of one method of handwriting over another; it does, however, indicate that D'Nealian-taught children produce fewer letter reversals (Koenke, 1986).

6. New letter forms have traditionally been taught through copying (Askov & Peck, 1982), and research comparing copying and tracing as instructional techniques has found copying to be superior, especially when verbal instruction is combined with demonstrations. Overlays have also been found to be useful (Askov & Peck, 1982).

7. Copying one letter does not generalize to another, so all letters must be taught individually (Askov & Peck, 1982).

8. Younger students using beginners' pencils do not produce better handwriting (Askov & Peck, 1982).

9. Research with wide-spaced paper has produced equivocable results (Askov & Peck, 1982; Koenke, 1986).

10. Research with LD students (Blandford & Lloyd, 1987; Kosiewicz, Hallahan, Lloyd, & Graves, 1982) has indicated that handwriting improves markedly if students are taught self-correction procedures. These procedures include questions the students can ask themselves about their handwriting and having them circle their own errors.

Multisensory Approaches to Handwriting

Research supports handwriting instruction that utilizes verbal cues to help children with letter formation. Furner (1969a, 1969b, 1970) described a series of steps to provide students with several exposures to a letter using multisensory (visual, auditory, and kinesthetic) techniques. In the first step, children are guided in observing how the teacher forms a letter, watching to see how many strokes the letter has (e.g., an "a" has two strokes), in what order the strokes are made (e.g., for "a," a circle and a line, the circle is made first), what direction the strokes are made in, and the size of the strokes. Next, children are asked to write the letter with one student verbally describing it; then they write it again while thinking of the verbal description. Furner's research supported the usefulness of these techniques. Research by Graham (1983) using similar techniques (verbal descriptions, modeling, and tracing) found the techniques to be useful for LD students.

Slingerland's *Multisensory Approach to Language Arts for Specific Language Disability Children* (Slingerland, 1971, 1976, 1981) includes a multisensory (V-A-K-T) sequence for teaching handwriting skills (Lesiak, 1984). A one-stroke manuscript is taught during the first 2 years of the program. Cursive writing is introduced in the third year. The verbal instructions for forming letters are much less complex than in Furner's approach (e.g., "h": down, up, and around) but seem sufficient. Tracing is an added cue. Forming large letters in the air, on the chalkboard, and on paper is a kinesthetic–tactile cue thought to help students remember the form of the letter. Detailed instructions are given in Slingerland's manuals for having students write on lined paper and produce rhythmic writing. Because the approach includes instruction in all of the language arts, handwriting is taught throughout the curriculum.

Slingerland and Aho (1985a, 1985b) outline procedures similar to those described in the Slingerland manuals for teaching manuscript and cursive writing.

The Orton–Gillingham approach (Gillingham & Stillman, 1973), designed primarily for students in grades 3 through 8, provides a multisensory approach to cursive writing instruction. Learning to write is linked to learning to spell and read. The student is led through a series of steps including watching the teacher form the letter, tracing the letter, copying the letter, writing without copy, and writing with eyes averted. The teacher can give verbal cues as he or she forms the letter. Instructions for the teacher are not as detailed as the instructions in the Slingerland manuals.

Review of A Handwriting Program

We have elected to review only one published handwriting program, the Scott, Foresman D'Nealian Handwriting Program (Thurber, 1978, 1981, 1987), because we believe it is one of the best programs for use with children who are having considerable difficulty learning to write. Many of the research findings noted earlier are included in the approach, and it lessens the difficulty of making the transition from manuscript to cursive. Instruction in the program can be supplemented with techniques borrowed from Slingerland. The program is designed for use in grades kindergarten through 8. Manuscript writing is taught in grades kindergarten, 1, and 2; the transition to cursive begins in grade 2.

Each D'Nealian manuscript letter is slanted and made with one stroke, with the exception of "f," "i," "j," "t," and "x," which require dots or crosses. Slant can be right, left, or vertical as long as it is consistent. D'Nealian manuscript letters were designed to ease the transition to cursive writing (Figure 9.2). Thurber suggests that the manuscript letters are 90% transferable to cursive. With the exception of the "f," "r," "s," "v," and "z," manuscript letters become cursive letters with the addition of simple joining strokes. Slant does not have to be learned for cursive writing because letters are taught on a slant from the beginning. The size of letters is controlled. For kindergarten, ⅝-inch ruled paper is used, and for grades 1–3, ½-inch ruled paper is used, thus avoiding continuous adjustments to changes in size. At fourth grade, a change is made to standard ⅓-inch ruled notebook paper. There are only three heights for letters: tall, small, and letters with descenders. Letters either fill the entire space, a half space, or a half space with a descender reaching a half space below the bottom line. Because children are taught to write words and phrases as soon as two or three letters are taught, spacing is taught from the beginning.

Other features of the program that make it an excellent choice for students with problems include the following:

- Instruction in letter forms includes verbal cues: " 'a': start at the middle line; curve down left to the bottom line; curve up right to the beginning, and close; retrace down and swing up," which is shortened to "middle start; around down, close up, down, and a monkey tail" (Thurber, 1987, manual grade 1, p. T36).
- Letters with dark lines emphasizing the strokes (a step-by-step visual sequence) are included for letter instruction.
- Stimulus letters appear at the beginning and end of practice lines for comparison and so that both right- and left-handed children can easily see the model.
- Tracing models are provided for the first few letters followed by starting dots.
- Individual letter practice is followed by practice in words and phrases once four letters have been taught.
- Practice exercises tend to emphasize functional writing.
- Students are taught to evaluate their writing.

FIGURE 9.2. D'Nealian handwriting, including lower-case manuscript and lower-case cursive writing. From *D'Nealian* ® *Handwriting* by Donald Thurber. Copyright © 1987 by Scott, Foresman and Company. Reprinted by permission.

Help with the Subskills of Handwriting

Letter Formation

If students still need practice with form despite being exposed to the procedures reviewed, use of a fading–tracing procedure is recommended. A sheaf of 10 or so pages of paper are separated by carbon paper. The teacher writes a page of the letter or letters with which the student has difficulty, resulting in faded images of the letter on succeeding practice pages (Frankel, 1976). The student proceeds through the pages with the aid of the teacher.

Letter Slant

Slant can be improved by slipping a paper with dark slant lines under the student's paper. The teacher can make his or her own slant paper or purchase it from A. N. Palmer, 1720 West Irving Park Road, Schaumburg, IL 60193.

Space

Graph paper, which comes in different sizes, can be used to improve spacing between letters and between words. When having students copy sentences, the teacher can mark between words in the sample because young students do not have a good concept of what a word is.

Alignment

Children are aided in alignment if the size of lined paper they use is consistent. Use of raised-line paper can also be helpful as it provides tactile feedback for errors; raised-line paper is available from the American Printing House for the Blind in Louisville, P.O. Box 6085 KY 40206 or from PRO-ED Publishing 8700 Shoal Creek Road, Austin, TX 78758.

Paper Slant

The appropriate slant of the paper can be aided by applying masking tape with the correct slant to the student's desk. The student can then use the tape as a guide. This is particularly important for left-handed students, because hooking the hand results in fatigue and smearing of writing.

Miscellaneous Tips We Have Found Helpful

- Pencils (regular sized) with soft lead are easier for students because marks appear on paper without undue pressure. The use of very short pencils should be avoided to insure proper pencil grip (i.e., about 1 inch from the tip).
- For the child just learning or the student who cannot remember or who confuses certain letters, a letter line taped to the desk serves as a cue to prevent mistakes.
- Teaching that a lower-case "b" is part of a capital "B" often helps eliminate the "b"/"d" confusion that results in reversals.
- Three-sided pencil grippers (available from Michigan Products, P.O. Box 24155, 1200 Keystone Avenue, Lansing, MI 48909-4155) are concrete aids to problems with pencil grip.

Alternatives to Handwriting

For some students, writing will always require too much time and effort. These students need to be taught alternatives to writing such as using typewriters and/or computers. Typewriters do not need to be fancy or new; donations can be sought from secondary schools, parents, or others in the community. The typewriter has several advantages over the computer: (1) old ones are often available free or at a nominal cost for both in-school and home use, and (2) the typewriter can be used for worksheets requiring lengthy responses. A systematic program for learning to use the typewriter (or computer) should be used, such as Keyboarding Skills (King, 1986).

SPELLING

The bad speller is nothing more nor less than one who, because of physical damage (rare) or shock and ill teaching (more common, I think), fixates at a primitive stage of word knowledge. He goes no further in his cognitive learning and, like all persons under stress, tries less and less effective strategies to cope with his problem. He tries mnemonic devices, spelling rules, spelling-by-sound, and the hopeless task of serial letter by letter memorization.

E. Henderson (1974, p. 178)

Reading, writing, and spelling are closely related: "Learning to spell is an aspect of general language development . . . much of an individual's knowledge about spelling . . . is learned throughout life by an interaction with written language" (i.e., reading and writing) (Hodges, 1982, p. 289). Henderson (1985) points out that children's first major source of information about correctly spelled words is the sight vocabulary of beginning reading materials; beginning readers note specific sequences of letters, which helps them learn to spell sight words. Students should not be expected to study words for spelling that they cannot read because they will soon forget these words. Words must be used to be retained.

Pupils must write frequently in order to be competent spellers (Beers & Beers, 1981; Gentry, 1982; Hillerich, 1985; Hodges, 1981), since spelling competency reflects exposure to words. Research by Beers and Beers (1981) indicates that students spell high-frequency words correctly almost twice as often as low-frequency words. "Effective spelling instruction must be embedded in whole-language experiences with meaningful practice and experimentation in both speech and writing" (Anderson, 1985, p. 145). Thus, it is important that the teacher provide daily purposeful writing experiences (Anderson, 1985; Gentry, 1982; Johnson, Langford, & Quorn, 1981). As Hillerich (1985) points out, "Spelling is needed only for writing" (p. 176). Daily writing allows students to practice their skills continually: "One learns to spell by spelling" (Hodges, 1981, p. 220). However, the emphasis must be on "purposeful writing" (writing that the student creates), not on copying words and sentences. "Copying sentences or words over and over provides little opportunity for children to use their knowledge about written words. Copiers do not have to think about what they are writing or how to write words, but merely execute correct eye–hand coordination" (Beers & Beers, 1981, p. 578). Daily writing is also a source of words that should be taught to the students; therefore, daily writing is important for both reinforcing spelling skills and building new spelling skills.

Research-Supported Practices

Fitzsimmons and Loomer (1977) reviewed more than 60 years of research in spelling and found certain "research-supported" procedures in spelling, which are listed and discussed below. The number in parentheses indicates the number of studies supporting each conclusion.

1. Presenting spelling words in list form is a more successful method than presenting spelling words in sentences or paragraph form (7 studies). Isolating the word allows the student to focus attention on it (Johnson et al., 1981).

2. The spelling words used most frequently in child and adult writing should be studied by elementary school children (7 studies). It

is logical for students to study words they will use frequently in the future. Hillerich (1978) found that five words ("I," "and," "the," "a," and "to") accounted for 18.2% of the running words used by students in grades 2 through 6 in writing. The 100 most frequently occurring words (Table 5.2) account for 60% of the words used by students in writing. These words are clearly important to teach.

Johnson et al. (1981) suggest that spelling words for instruction come from (1) words for which students ask the spelling; (2) words that students misspell in their daily writing activities; and (3) words that the teacher knows the student will need to spell.

3. The major contribution of spelling games is the stimulation of pupil interest (3 studies). Games may stimulate interest in spelling, but they should not be used in place of instruction.

4. Correcting his or her own spelling test, under the direction of the teacher, is the single most important task for the student learning to spell (8 studies). Henderson (1985) suggests that if the student is being taught at an appropriate level of difficulty, this self-correction may be sufficient for learning to spell.

Important to self-correction is proofreading. We need to encourage proofreading and editing in student writing (Beers & Beers, 1981; Gentry, 1982; Hillerich, 1985; Johnson et al., 1981; Schell, 1975): "The ultimate reason for teaching spelling is that the knowledge and skill gained during the spelling period, can and will be used in all writing situations. . . . Unless improvement of spelling in other writing situations occurs, spelling instruction has been meaningless and futile" (Schell, 1975, p. 239). Teachers need to provide time for proofreading, correcting, and recopying: "Proofreading must be an integral part of instruction so that it is perceived by pupils as being important" (Schell, 1975, p. 241). Schell suggests that proofing for spelling errors be a separate step in the proofreading process and that procedures be established for correction (e.g., ask the teacher or another student, consult a chart of frequently misspelled words, consult a misspeller's dictionary).

Schell (1975) lists several activities that can be used to encourage proofreading for misspellings: (1) "Catch the Teacher," where the teacher writes on the chalkboard purposely misspelling words for the students to catch; and (2) awarding students for proofreading with certificates such as "Most Diligent," "Keenest Eye," "Certificate of Merit for Proofreading Achievement," signed by "Ima Goodspeller."

The overall goal is the development of a "spelling conscience" (Hillerich, 1985); it is important that students learn that correct spelling is a courtesy to the reader.

5. Children do not have to learn the meaning of the majority of

their spelling words (3 studies). While this may be true, it makes spelling an end in itself rather than a means to communication. It is doubtful that students will use words they do not understand in their writing; therefore, words students are taught should be those the student understands.

6. Spelling lists derived from various curricular areas are of little value in increasing spelling ability (6 studies). This conclusion is linked to research with high-frequency words. Subject-specific words add little to a student's functional spelling vocabulary; words are typically forgotten and not used when, for example, the science unit has ended.

7. Learning words by the whole method is better than learning words by syllables (3 studies). In addition, research did not support having students look at "hard spots" in a word to improve spelling (four studies). Johnson et al. (1981) suggest that the "chaining hypothesis" best accounts for the effectiveness of whole-word teaching: "In writing down the beginning of the word the necessary muscular movements and the resultant visual image combine to produce a stimulus that triggers off the next response which in turn becomes a stimulus" (p. 585). The chaining hypothesis also suggests that writing words in the air (using large muscles as opposed to those used in writing) and oral letter-by-letter spelling (no visual image) have little value in teaching spelling. However, the chaining hypothesis alone does not account for spelling because research indicates that writing words over and over is not effective in itself because writing the words becomes mechanical (Beers & Beers, 1981; Henderson, 1985; Johnson et al., 1981): "The practice of requiring children to write misspelled words ten times each is a bad practice. Repetitions in that number do not reinforce recall. They fatigue the hand, numb attention, promote error, and actually block the very memory mechanisms which it was hoped they might support. It need scarcely be added that writing a word one hundred times is a mild form of torture suitable, perhaps, for the wicked, but not for teaching them to spell" (Henderson, 1985, p. 90).

8. Due to the nature of the English language, most attempts to teach spelling by phonic rules are questionable (13 studies). This finding may appear illogical in the face of certain studies of the English language (Chomsky & Halle, 1968; Hanna et al., 1966; Venezky, 1967). For example, Hanna et al. (1966) found that 50% of 17,000 words could be spelled correctly on the basis of common sound–letter factors. In addition, 37% of the misspelled words had only one incorrect grapheme–phoneme match, and most of these misspellings could be accounted for by morphological factors

(Hodges, 1982). Thus, it can be seen that phonics is only a part of spelling: "Researchers agree that phonics should be part of spelling instruction, but that it should not be the entire program" (Lehr, 1984, p. 218).

Johnson et al. (1981) point out that teaching generalizations is a good example of confusing teaching with learning, since generalizations are learned through multiple experiences with words; teachers need to draw students' attentions to spelling patterns, but "it is a mistake to teach generalizations" (Johnson et al., 1981, p. 586). Other writers seem to concur with Johnson et al. (Anderson, 1985; Beers & Beers, 1981; Henderson, 1985; Hodges, 1982). One notable exception is Hillerich (1985), who believes that words should be taught using "a good word list" with words grouped randomly, that is, not by patterns, balancing for difficulty.

Most new spelling series present words that follow similar patterns together. Johnson et al. (1981) suggest that when similar words are presented together (e.g., "ook" words), the student gives minimal attention to the repeated phonogram. Beers and Beers (1981) present an alternative that can be used periodically with any spelling program; they suggest having students classify a known list of words under various headings (e.g., short vowel words, long vowel words, verbs endings in "ing," etc.). Then the following questions are discussed: Why did you put these words together? What do you find similar or different about these words? Why is this a useful category?

9. Time allotted for the study of spelling should be between 1 hour and 75 minutes per week (3 studies). This time allotment is for the formal study of spelling and should be separated into daily sessions of 10–15 minutes. Research on learning supports distributed practice for rote learning.

10. The test–study method is superior to the study–test method when working with most students (10 studies). That is, students should only be studying words they do not know!

Research has also indicated that students need to be taught a systematic approach for studying each word; that is, the research did not support having students devise their own individual method of study (six studies). Recent research with LD subjects supports previous research. For example, Graham and Freeman (1986) found that students who were taught a five-step strategy for word study recalled significantly more spelling words than a group simply instructed to study the list of words.

Graham and Miller (1986) present several strategies for studying the spelling of words. The procedures vary primarily in how much emphasis is put on saying the word (e.g., simply say the word or say the letters in the word) and how much writing of the word is done (e.g., no writing or word written ten times over several steps). An example is provided below:

Fitzgerald Method
1. Look at the word carefully.
2. Say the word.
3. With eyes closed, visualize the word.
4. Cover the word and then write it.
5. Check the spelling.
6. If the word is misspelled, repeat steps 1–5.

The method utilized in the study by Graham and Freeman (1986) involves tracing the word:

1. Say the word.
2. Write and say the word.
3. Check the word.
4. Trace and say the word.
5. Write the word from memory and check.
6. Repeat the first five steps.

Graham and Miller (1986) suggest that since no one method of study has been shown to be the most effective for all individuals, the teacher can select one and, if that doesn't work for a particular student, try another.

Spelling Instruction

Most writers appear to agree that formal spelling instruction using lists or books has an important place in the spelling curriculum but should be supplemented with informal instruction (instruction as a part of writing activities). According to Henderson (1985), "Formal instruction provides the basic knowledge; informal instruction teaches the skills, habits, and understandings necessary for an independent mastery of the full vocabulary" (p. 168). Formal instruction provides knowledge about words. Hillerich (1985) points out that "automatic spelling vocabulary is too important to be left to chance, and we know that incidental spelling instruction is accidental spelling instruction" (p. 181).

Hodges (1982) points out that despite recent research in spelling, there are "many unresolved issues remaining, most notably with regard to the development of a spelling curriculum itself" (p. 289). At the present time, we feel that research in spelling supports the following characteristics of a "formal" spelling program:

1. Students must be able to read the words. For beginning readers and older readers with limited reading ability, we suggest that formal spelling utilize words from the reading program, in particular, words that are high frequency for spelling. For reading programs that focus on teaching words as wholes (i.e., as sight words), initial instruction might focus on the 100 most frequently used words in writing. Most of these words are also high frequency for reading.
2. Words should be taught as wholes; the words taught should be words used frequently in writing (i.e., high-frequency words).
3. Words should be isolated for instruction.
4. Students need exposure to spelling patterns so they can learn about words. Henderson (1985) points out that "the most consistent and frequently occurring pattern is that for the short vowel, and that pattern requires particular attention because the vowel phoneme is represented differently than children expect. It is for this reason that the short vowel patterns need to be studied first and very carefully" (pp. 120–121).
5. Students need to be taught a step-by-step study strategy.
6. Activities that encourage meaningful practice of words in writing are important. Graves (1976) reviewed research by Cohen (1969) indicating that some activities in published materials are not appropriate for spelling instruction and may even be "deterrents" to learning. Cohen's research indicated that students in grades 5 and 6 spelled better when given exercises that required using the word in a meaningful way (e.g., in a phrase or sentence) as opposed to exercises stressing homophones, attention to affixes and inflectional endings, etc. Cohen's review of nine spelling series from 1955 to 1961 and Grave's review of nine series from 1970 to 1976) indicated an emphasis on word study exercises rather than word usage. Other activities we have noted in spelling series that do not appear valuable for students with spelling problems include word searches, filling in configuration boxes, filling in missing letters, and unscrambling letters.
7. Only 10–15 minutes per day need be spent on formal instruction.
8. Students should correct their own papers.

Reviews of Spelling Programs

For reading or language arts programs that stress phonics, instruction in spelling will focus initially on words that are phonetically regular. The multisensory approaches (Gillingham & Stillman, 1973; Slingerland, 1971, 1976, 1981) discussed in the handwriting section also teach spelling. In both of these methods, particularly the Orton-Gillingham, there is an emphasis on learning rules of spelling, but students are not expected to state those rules in the Slingerland approach. Rudginsky and Haskell (1984) developed a formal spelling program based on the Orton-Gillingham approach, *How to Teach Spelling*. The program is best used in grades 3 through 8 but can also be used in grades 1–12. Although some sight words are taught, the emphasis is on learning to spell words correctly by relying on spelling rules and generalizations. Lessons emphasize writing from dictation, including nonsense syllables, words, phrases, and sentences.

When students' reading abilities reach a second-grade level and short vowels have been introduced, published spelling series can be selected for formal instruction or graded lists can be used. Reviewing all of the series available for spelling instruction is beyond the scope of this chapter; however, it is recommended that teachers select series that teach high-frequency words, acquaint students with word patterns, and provide meaningful practice writing words.

Two series we have reviewed in depth and found to be useful are Teaching Resources Spelling Series (Packard & Rybicki, 1983) and Spelling Workout (Trocki, 1985). Both of these series can be used with older students.

The Teaching Resources Spelling Series is designed for students in grades 3–8. The three levels, A, B, and C, are written on reading levels 2, 3, and 4, respectively. Each text contains 30 weekly lessons (generally 2–3 pages each) and two or three review lessons. Words for study, generally 12–15 per lesson, consist of patterned words (80%) and sight words (20%); they are generally high-frequency words. Activities in the books are varied, most requiring the student to use a word in a meaningful manner. Some activities (e.g., unscrambling letters to make words) should be skipped. The program does not present a method for word study, but such a method can be taught by the teacher. Each week, a letter is sent to parents requesting that they help students "memorize" the words for the week; however, it is recommended that this be skipped and students be taught a study method.

Spelling Workout is a six-book series designed for use in grades 1 through 6; however, its sports format makes it particularly useful for older students. Each weekly lesson (36 per book) provides a "coach" (male or female) to teach and motivate. The coach explains the spelling pattern under study. Students progress through a variety of activities under such headings as "Pep Talks" and "The Big Game." While some of the activities are useful (e.g., writing words for riddles, completing sentences using the words, proofreading), others should be skipped (e.g., writing words in configuration boxes, unscrambling letters to write words) and replaced by teacher-designed activities. Words misspelled on the final weekly test are placed in a "word locker." After five lessons are completed, there is a review ("Instant Replay"); one section requires students to "clean out your locker"—to study words misspelled in previous lessons. The most useful levels of the program are A–D because they use a large number of high-frequency words (96%, 84%, 81%, and 46%, respectively, using the Fitzgerald list). Levels E and F teach only 30% high-frequency words.

Because both series present words grouped by patterns, it is recommended that students be given periodic lessons in which they use the words learned and sort them into groups using the procedures suggested by Beers and Beers (1981) discussed earlier. This can be an individual or group activity.

Spelling Lists

An alternative or adjunct to a book program is the use of graded spelling lists. Hillerich (1985) has developed lists for grades 2 through 8. The lists were drawn from four word lists, two from printed materials and two based on children's writing. Hillerich states that students who learn the words and their regularly inflected forms will be able to spell 98% of words written by children and adults. Teaching only the grade 2 words will result in a spelling vocabulary of 70% of words usually used in writing. An analysis of the words using the Fitzgerald list indicated that words for grades 2 through 5 are generally of high frequency (98%, 96%, 89%, and 74%, respectively). Lists for grades 6, 7, and 8 contain relatively few words appearing on the Fitzgerald list. Words on the lists are coded as to the percentage of pupils (from approximately 500 per grade) who missed the word, giving an indication of difficulty. Hillerich suggests that words for weekly study be selected so that the students have words of differing levels of difficulty. In our opinion, the teacher should provide written activities for practice writing the words in context.

Compensatory Devices

Students whose spelling skills severely limit their ability to express themselves in writing need to be taught to use compensatory devices, at least on a temporary basis. Directing students to "look up the word in the dictionary" is not appropriate; it is very difficult to look up a word for which one does not know the spelling! As indicated earlier, students can circle words they are unsure of as they write them, then look them up using one or more of the procedures that follow. A crucial point, however, is that the student must recognize his or her inability to spell the word. This is a problem for some poor spellers, especially in the case of homonyms. The following are a few suggestions to aid students:

1. Students can keep a notebook of high-frequency words and words they frequently misspell for reference. Words could be alphabetized with tabbed pages.

2. A misspellers' dictionary is useful. We have found *How to Spell It* (Wittels & Greisman, 1982) to be one of the best misspellers' books available for students of any age.

3. A new minicomputer device (slightly larger than a calculator) that we highly recommend is the Franklin Spelling Ace, which has a dictionary of 88,000 words. The student enters a word and waits for the computer to check it. If the word is correct, the computer signals that it is; if it is not correct, a list is provided of words that are spelled similarly. It is even possible to enter only the beginning letters of a word followed by a hyphen, with a list of possible words then made available.

These three items are all portable. In addition, students can be taught how to use spelling checkers on computers. It is important to select a spelling program that has a sufficient number of words in its dictionary and that allows the writer to add words of his or her own (e.g., slang) (Betza, 1987). As with other devices, spelling checkers cannot detect misuses of homonyms.

COMPOSITION

> *Research on the composing process indicates that writing is an enormously complex task, demanding the use of at least four types of knowledge: knowledge of the content to be written about; procedural knowledge that enables the manipulation of content; knowledge of discourse structures, including the schemata underlying various types of writing (e.g., story, argument), syntactic forms, and the conventions of punctuation and usage; and the procedural knowledge that enables the production of a piece of writing of a particular type.* G.Hillocks (1987, p. 73)

As noted earlier, students learn to write by writing. This principle appears over and over in the literature. Hillocks (1987) points out that the complexity of writing indicates that current school instructional practices are inadequate. Most writing exercises given to students require short answers or perhaps a paragraph or two; such short assignments hamper the development of the capacity to plan and write more extensively on a topic. These instructional procedures also do not teach students that writing involves making changes (i.e., editing, revising) (Hillocks, 1987). Some teachers "solve" this problem by requiring students to produce a research paper once or twice a year. Kean (1981) points out that "shorter, regular opportunities to write are probably much more productive than the massive burst of energy required to produce a term paper once a semester" (p. 175).

Research on Instructional Practices

Hillocks's review (1987) of approximately 2,000 research studies examined six instructional focuses. Results of the review are summarized below.

Grammar

"The study of traditional school grammar (i.e., the definition of parts of speech, the parsing of sentences, etc.) has no effect on raising the quality of student writing" (Hillocks, 1987, p. 76). Straw (1981) argues that grammar lessons are not influential because they involve taking sentences apart, which is not what writing is about. "Grammar study should be incorporated within the writing program rather than taught separately. It should be taught on a need-to-know basis when the writing that students are doing calls for it" (Kean, 1981, p. 175). However, these procedures will only work if students write frequently.

Models

"The presentation of good pieces of writing as models is significantly more useful than the study of grammar" (Hillocks, 1987, p. 76). However, although presenting models has merit, the use of models alone is not sufficient. Hillocks suggest that this may be because students are asked to imitate the models rather than to produce writing with certain characteristics.

Sentence Combining

"The practice of building complex sentences from simple ones has been shown to be effective in a large number of experimental studies. . . . [It is] more than twice as effective as free writing as a means of enhancing the quality of student writing" (Hillocks, 1987, p. 76). Sentence combining (SC) helps students develop a repertoire of structures for writing. Straw (1981) argues that SC builds on what is known about language and more closely resembles the synthetic nature of language processing; it aids students "in handling and expressing ideas . . . better, more clearly, and more maturely" (Straw, 1981, p. 157). Strong (1986) presents a comprehensive review of research on the effectiveness of SC activities. Based on his review he generates ten assumptions that appear to underlie the SC approach.

1. SC is not real writing. . . . Exercises are no substitute for naturalistic (real writing) experiences. . . . SC is a skill-building adjunct.
2. SC is not a model of the composing process. . . . [It] pertains to revision and editing [and] *can* serve as a writing springboard when students enter an exercise imaginatively.
3. SC exercises come in two basic varieties: cued (or signaled) and open (usually whole-discourse) exercises.
4. SC is one approach to improved syntactic fluency. . . . The aim . . . is to make good sentences, not merely long ones.
5. SC instruction assumes that mistakes are a natural, inevitable, and desirable part of language learning.
6. SC instruction should move from oral rehearsal to written transcription.
7. SC can be used to teach virtually any language/composition concept inductively.
8. SC requires that teachers model editing and decision-making skills with students. . . . Mindless combining—without instructional focus or follow-up work—will soon prove boring. . . . Too much SC ruins its appeal.
9. SC is mainly a synthetic process, not an analytic [one]. Sooner or later, however, analysis plays a role—as in decombining of overly complex texts.
10. SC works best when done two or three times a week for short periods, when students use exercises as springboards for journals or controlled writing, when teachers and students monitor problem sentences, and when transfer is made to real writing—either through decombined student drafts or marginal notations (From *Creative Approaches to Sentence Combining*, by W. Strong, 1986, pp. 21–22; reprinted with permission of the National Council of Teachers of English).

Strong's book provides numerous practice activities in sentence combining. Activities are coded G (general), E (elementary), or MS (middle school). The text ends with a list of 20 teaching suggestions (e.g., "discuss the purpose of SC—to make good sentences, not necessarily long ones"). We highly recommend this book.

Scales

"Scales, criteria, and specific questions that students apply to their own or others' writing have a powerful effect on enhancing quality" (Hillocks, 1987, p. 76). Giving students questions to ask about their writing or criteria to judge their writing improves writing quality.

Inquiry

Focusing students' attention on strategies for transforming raw data (e.g., looking for explanatory generalizations, forming arguments to defend a position, finding details that convey experience) is on the average "three-and-a-half times more effective than free writing and over two-and-a-half times more effective than" studying models (Hillocks, 1987, p. 76).

Free Writing

Although free writing is more effective than teaching grammar in improving the quality of writing, it is less effective than the other procedures. Hillocks (1987), however, feels it has a place in writing instruction if integrated with other techniques. Dagenais and Beadle (1984) point out that writing in and of itself does not necessarily improve quality—there is still a need for guided instruction.

In addition to the review provided by Hillocks (1987), Dagenais and Beadle (1984) cite research to support that positive, nonjudgmental teacher or peer feedback regarding clarity of ideas or mechanical aspects is related to improvement in writing.

Motivating Students to Write

Students with difficulties in written expression often have negative attitudes and are often apprehensive about writing (Auten, 1983). Auten (1983) cites several studies that indicate that the writing of apprehensive students is of lesser quality than that of other students. Therefore, it is crucial that attention be given to students' attitudes toward writing. Suggestions for reducing student apprehension and increasing motivation follow.

1. Veit (cited in Auten, 1983) suggests that teachers create anxiety about writing through teaching practices—in particular, requiring students to write under pressure for a grade. He suggests that teachers can reduce anxiety by changing grading procedures (e.g., not grading the first attempt, being positive rather than negative) and showing enthusiasm for writing.

2. Free writing or journal writing on topics of self-interest is often suggested as a way to reduce anxiety and increase motivation (Auten, 1983). Most authors view free writing/journal writing as a prelude to finished papers on particular topics. Journals should not be graded. If students have difficulty writing in a journal, a class journal can be used at first, with students eventually moving to individual journals.

3. Writing papers (as opposed to free writing) on topics of interest is important (Gaskins, 1982; Green & Petty, 1975). "Children cannot be taught to write effectively, to improve their writing, unless attention is given to their interests, their experiences, and their sense of satisfaction or value in actual writing" (Greene & Petty, 1975, p. 287). Freeman and Sanders (1987) argue that most writing in schools is in response to a teacher's goals or objectives, that school writing is separate from "real writing": "If students could feel that their writing serves a function relevant to their lives and interests perhaps they would be more willing to work on their writing tasks until the writing is truly completed and not merely handed over to the authorities" (Freeman & Sanders, 1987, p. 644).

4. Positive interactions with the teacher and with other students about writing (peer sharing/editing) encourage students to write more (Gaskins, 1982; Graves, 1983).

The principles of writing instruction and the procedures outlined for teaching writing that follow take these ideas into consideration.

General Procedures for Teaching Composition

Graham and Harris (1988) outline ten recommendations for teaching writing to students with difficulties. We view these recommendations as important principles for teaching composition.

1. *Allocate time for writing instruction.* As mentioned previously, researchers stress that students learn to write by writing. Following an analysis of errors and strategies used in writing by LD students, Thomas et al. (1987) concluded that LD students must have time to write. They must be involved in sustained writing opportunities rather than just sentence writing or worksheet activities. Graham and Harris (1988) recommend that students write at least four times per week. Bos (1988) cites 45 minutes per day, pointing out that students need to learn that a piece does not have to be finished in one sitting. However, providing time is not sufficient for teaching writing; carefully designed instructional programs with practice in developing skills are also necessary.

2. *Expose students to a broad range of writing tasks.* These activities should develop skills necessary for completing school assignments and for meeting social, recreational, and occupational needs.

3. *Create a social climate conducive to writing development.* The teacher must be accepting and supportive, and sharing and collaboration among students should be encouraged. Bos (1988) refers to this as creating a "writing community."

4. *Integrate writing with other academic subjects.* Writing should be taught across the curriculum. "The careful integration of writing and other language arts activities can result in more writing and serve as a bridge for developing writing skills" (Graham & Harris, 1988, p. 508). It is important, however, that this not be used as a substitute for separate instruction in writing.

5. *Aid students in developing the processes central to effective writing.* Graham and Harris point out that dividing composition into discrete stages (e.g., prewrite, write, and rewrite) helps students develop writing processes. "The process of writing at the very least entails first thinking about a topic, deciding how to express one's thoughts, setting down one's thoughts as text, and working with the text as well as one's thoughts to create a complete and final representation of what one wishes to say" (Aulls, 1981, p. 273). Poor writers spend less time with the process of writing (Aulls, 1981; Stoddard, 1987) and therefore need instruction here. Students need to learn that "writing is a process, not just a product" (Stoddard, 1987, p. 17). (The steps in the writing process are discussed in more detail later.)

6. *Automatize skills (i.e., mechanics of writing) for getting language onto paper.* These skills (e.g., handwriting, spelling) should be taught separately from composition.

7. *Help students develop explicit knowledge about the characteristics of different types of good writing.* More research is needed in this area; however, some research suggests that modeling (with practice and feedback in imitating the model) and direct instruction are useful techniques for students with learning problems. Englert and Raphael (1988) report a writing program under study—Cognitive Strategy Instruction in Writing—that utilizes modeling and direct instruction. The program "focuses on teaching writing strategies through the use of think-alouds that model cognitions that underlie each writing subprocess (planning, drafting, editing, and revising)" (pp. 517–518).

8. *Help students develop the skills and abilities to carry out more sophisticated composing processes.* Students should pursue goals slightly beyond their current capabilities. Procedures suggested by Graham and Harris (1988) include conferencing, where the teacher acts as a collaborator by giving hints or prompts or by providing strategy instruc-

tion. As an example of the latter, Harris and Graham (1985) found that self-control strategy training increased the use of action words, action helpers, and describing words by two LD students. A five-step strategy for writing good stories was introduced as part of a cognitive behavior modification procedure. These steps included the following: (a) looking at the picture and writing down good action words; (b) thinking of a good story idea in which to use the words; (c) writing a story that makes sense and uses good action words; (d) reading the story and asking if it is good and if it uses action words; and (3) fixing the story, possibly by using more action words.

9. *Assist students in the development of goals for improving their written products.* This includes having students evaluate their own writing according to specific criteria and using peer evaluation.

10. *Avoid instructional practices that do not improve students' writing performance.* Examples of these include diagramming sentences and teaching parts of speech.

Teaching the Writing Process

Gaskins (1982) outlined a three-step procedure for teaching writing: before writing, during writing, and after writing. In these steps, "the student writes, the teacher and peers react, and the student decides and revises" (Gaskins, 1982, p. 860). The procedures outlined by Gaskins are similar to those described by Graves (1983) and Bos (1988). Bos refers to this as "process-oriented writing." Gaskins emphasizes the point that no one, adult or student, writes without information.

It is important to allow students to select a topic in which they have an interest and about which they know something. Part of the before-writing stage is selecting a topic. Other students (or the teacher in some cases) interview the "experts" to give the students doing the writing some ideas. The before-writing time can also include the search for other facts needed to write. Whitt, Paul, and Reynolds (1988) suggest that this stage include devising a semantic map or an outline for ideas to be covered. The necessity of this stage—and the extent to which it is developed—depends on the type of writing involved. For example, writing about a favorite television program requires less planning than writing an autobiography.

For students who never have anything to write about, provide a bulletin board with possible topics. Hillerich (1985) provides an extensive listing of titles in a variety of categories (e.g., fact or fiction, personal, how-to) selected from the writings of students of various ages. For students who write regularly on one topic, Bos (1988) and

Graves (1983) suggest that areas of interest can be broadened by having those students listen to other students or through teacher modeling on how to select a topic.

The during-writing stage is also called "cheerleading and coaching." The teacher circulates and responds in positive ways to what the student is writing. Coaching is done in response to a student's need or request for help. Students are encouraged to reread their writing as they write, with a look to possible revision. Bos (1988) refers to this as the "drafting" stage.

During the after-writing stage, others react to the rough draft and the student edits and revises. Bos (1988) divides this stage into a "revising and editing" stage and "sharing and publication" stage. Three possible sources of reaction to the rough draft are individual teacher comments, class discussion, and individual or small peer-group editing conferences; conferences are viewed by most writers in the field as the best sources of reaction. Graves (1983) provides many examples of "questions that teach" and examples of student–teacher dialogue during individual conferences. Gaskins (1982) suggests four aspects of writing for student consideration: (a) thought content: the value of the ideas expressed and extent of development; (b) organization: the flow of ideas and the logic with which they are developed; (c) effectiveness: the clarity of expression, including use of precise vocabulary and originality; and (d) mechanics: capitalization, punctuation, spelling, and grammar (p. 859).

Gaskins emphasizes positive feedback (i.e., feedback in an "approving atmosphere"), using comments that encourage (e.g., "super," "well done") and give guidance for improving writing. Graham and Harris (1988) point out that it is important not to overemphasize errors; they suggest pinpointing only one or two types of errors at any one time, giving priority to errors that occur frequently and obstruct the reader's understanding of the text. Positive feedback can be emphasized during peer conferences by having the other students first state what they liked about the writing. Bos (1988) suggests establishing rules for providing feedback (e.g., start with a helpful suggestion) and allowing the student to call on peers. Students who are consistently negative should not be called on until they learn to begin on a positive note.

Graves (1983) and Bos (1988) suggest that teachers keep a writing folder for each student. The folder can include current writing projects, a list of finished works, ideas for future topics, writing goals, and mechanical aids (e.g., lists of capitalization or punctuation rules).

Research with process-oriented approaches for students with learning problems is limited (Bos, 1988). Bos points out that "teachers working with exceptional students should be encouraged by process-oriented approaches for teaching writing, but at the same time should see the need for systematic research" (p. 526). The Cognitive Strategy Instruction in Writing Program mentioned earlier (Englert & Raphael, 1988) holds promise for students with learning problems. The program utilizes steps similar to those described here but includes more dialogue with the teacher and "think sheets," which guide students as they write.

Reviews of Remedial Methods for Teaching Composition Skills

The Fitzgerald Key (Fitzgerald, 1966; Phelps-Gunn & Phelps-Terasaki, 1982), a method developed for use with the hearing impaired, is useful for teaching all students who experience difficulties in sentence writing. The key provides visual cues to language. A series of categories is presented to cue words to construct sentences (e.g., whose/who/what, verb symbol, where: John is running to the store). The method can be adapted for use with students who tend to write short sentences. For example, "John is running to the store" can be expanded with the category "how": John is running to the store fast—or with "why": John is running to the store to buy a loaf of bread. Joann Fokes has developed a series of programs based on the Fitzgerald Key using pictures (available from DLM/Teaching Resources, P.O. Box 4000, One DLM Park, Allen, TX 75002). The Fokes Sentence Builder (Fokes, 1976) and Fokes Sentence Builder Expansion (Fokes, 1977) were developed as oral language programs but can be used for both oral and written language development. The Fokes Written Language Program (Fokes, 1982) is designed for the middle- to upper-elementary grades.

Sentences and Other Systems (Blackwell, Engen, Fischgrund, & Zarcadoolas, 1978; Phelps-Gunn & Phelps-Terasaki, 1982) was designed as an alternative to the Fitzgerald Key to teach oral and written language skills to hearing-impaired students. Rather than beginning with isolated words and moving to sentences as in the Fitzgerald method, instruction is initiated with sentences. The program teaches students to use five kernel sentences (subject + verb; subject + verb + object; subject + state of being or linking verb + adjective; subject + state of being or linking verb + predicate noun; subject + state of being linking verb + adverb). Once these are learned, different words can be substituted to write different sentences. Traditional grammar instruction follows (e.g., labeling units of a sentence). This is followed by expanding the kernel sentences into more complex sentences and "tree" diagramming the sentences. As students progress in the program, instruction is provided in writing paragraphs and longer selections. Journal writing is encouraged.

As indicated earlier, research generally does not support a focus on labeling parts of speech or diagramming sentences. Phelps-Gunn and Phelps-Terasaki (1982) point out that, once students learn to write kernel sentences, they can be taught to "stretch them out" to contain more information without learning grammar or tree diagramming. Phelps-Gunn and Phelps-Terasaki (1982) also point out that the approach may not be suitable for students whose oral language skills exceed their written language skills.

The Phelps Sentence Guide Program (Phelps-Gunn & Phelps-Terasaki, 1982) began as another adaptation of the Fitzgerald Key but has been modified and expanded to nine stages, beginning with the sentence and progressing to paragraphs and stories. This guide is "a visual system of structuring sentences using an interactive teacher–child dialogue that emphasizes components and their interface and communicative function in the sentence, requires repetition and practice in whole sentence units, and steadily builds written competency at each stage without overwhelming the pupil by the complexity of the task" (Phelps-Gunn & Phelps-Terasaki, 1982, p. 101).

Another program designed to teach students to write basic sentence structures is Apple Tree (Anderson, Boren, Caniglia, Howard, & Krohn, 1980) (Dormac, PO Box 752, Beaverton, OR). Although the program was designed for hearing-impaired and multiply-handicapped students, it can be used with any student with language deficiency problems. The basic program consists of six student workbooks, a teacher's manual, and a test. Five teaching strategies are used in the program.

1. Comprehension: Understanding of the vocabulary, as well as concepts and the form of structure, is developed.
2. Manipulation: Students manipulate words or phrases in order to develop an awareness that certain words fit into specific positions in a sentence.
3. Substitution: One variable is used at a time to enable to student to move from the known to the unknown.
4. Production: The student writes after he or she has comprehended and internalized the structure form so effectively that it can be produced spontaneously.
5. Transformation: Rearrangements are made in simple sentence patterns, such as changing a declarative sentence into a question.

Before initiating the program, the teacher must be certain that students have an adequate meaningful vocabulary base (suggestions for developing vocabulary are given in the manual). Once a basic vocabulary is established, the teacher then uses the processes of sub-stitution, controlled composition (completing multiple-choice sen-tences), manipulation, and short stories to develop readiness for the workbooks further. Ten basic language structures are taught in the program (e.g., N_1 + V(be) + adj: "The man is tall." N_1 + V + N_3 + N_2: "Jerry sent me a card.") The student workbooks are used in conjunction with the suggestions in the teacher's manual to *reinforce* concepts taught or to evaluate mastery of the concepts. Activities in the books vary, progressing from easy to difficult and moving from writing a word or phrase to writing complete sentences. The manual provides activities and teaching suggestions for each of the basic language structures.

Reviews of Selected Materials for Teaching Composition Skills

Materials that we have reviewed and found to be of value in teaching composition skills are summarized and critiqued in this section. We feel these materials should be incorporated into broader-based pro-grams that use ideas expressed previously; that is, the materials should be adjuncts to interactive teacher–student programs.

Expressive Writing I and II

Expressive Writing (Engelmann & Silbert, 1985; available from C. C. Publications, PO Box 23699, Tigard, OR 97223-0108) is a direct-instruction approach to teaching composition skills; lessons are scripted with teacher modeling and student responses in a stimulus–response format. Expressive Writing I, designed for students who have not had previous instruction in expressive writing and who read on a third-grade level, "teaches the most fundamental rules about translating observations into sentences, about writing paragraphs that do not deviate from a topic, and about editing the works of others as well as one's own work" (Teacher Presentation Book, p. 1). Expressive Writing II is for students who have completed Expressive Writing I or who can read at a beginning fourth-grade level, read and write cursive, copy simple sentences at the rate of 15 words per minute, and write in a way that shows an understanding of appropriate language patterns. The preprogram for Expressive Writing II teaches the rules for creating simple declarative sentences. The regular program fo-cuses on "Writing clearly . . . writing with a variety of sentences . . . writing what people say . . . editing for clarity, punctuation, para-graphs and sentence forms" (Teacher Presentation Book, p. 1). Com-ponents of the program include a teacher's presentation book and student workbook at each level.

Expressive Writing I contains 50 lessons, each generally taking 45 minutes to complete. Specific skills taught are organized in four tracks: (1) mechanics (copying accurately, reading passages written in cursive, capitalizing the first word in a sentence and putting a period at the end of the sentence, indenting the first word of a paragraph); (2) sentence writing (identifying the subject and predicate of a sentence, completing or writing sentences that refer to pictured scenes, writing a title sentence); (3) paragraph writing (completing paragraphs that refer to pictured scenes; writing paragraphs that report on an individual in an illustration, tell about a series of things an individual did in a sequence of pictures, and interpret what must have happened between pictures in a sequence); and (4) editing (identifying sentences that do not report on what a picture shows; correcting mistakes in capitalization and punctuation; identifying sentences in a passage that do not tell about a specific topic; correcting run-on sentences, etc.).

Expressive Writing II contains 10 preprogram lessons and 45 lessons. Specific skills taught include (1) mechanics (review of those taught in Expressive Writing I; punctuating sentences that begin with a dependent clause or that list actions or names; punctuating compound sentences that use the word "but" and have direct quotes; and paragraphing passages with direct quotes); (2) sentence writing (review of Expressive Writing I; writing sentences that begin with dependent clauses, those that list, and those that use quotations); (3) paragraph and story writing (writing passages that report on events illustrated in pictures, that infer events not shown in pictures, and that include direct quotes; and completing imaginative stories); and (4) editing (similar to Expressive Writing I).

Lessons are graded in difficulty and are presented in detail in the presentation books with explicit directions (or scripts) for the teacher. Daily lessons (or at least three lessons a week) are recommended. Students respond as a group after the teacher gives a signal (e.g., handclap or snap of fingers) or on an individual basis. Lessons contain several tasks (drawn from the four tracks) to complete together or independently. All work is corrected or checked during the lesson. When students are working independently, the teacher is expected to move around checking work and giving appropriate feedback. Suggested comments are given in the manual. Beginning in Lesson 6 in Expressive Writing I, "check" questions are printed to remind students to check their work after finishing writing a paragraph. In Expressive Writing II, a point system is used to encourage students to check their work.

Students respond to activities in the workbook or on lined paper.

For lessons that require independent writing, words the student might use are presented in a "vocabulary box."

Expressive Writing is an excellent program for students in the upper-elementary grades with disabilities in written expression that center on composing sentences, paragraphs, or both. Lessons move from instruction to guided practice to independent writing. Students do independent writing activities in all lessons and are taught to monitor their work. However, we recommend that the copying activities be skipped as they have little merit in improving composition skills.

English, Inc.

English, Inc., Language Skills for Effective Writing (Berke, 1981; available from Reader's Digest/Random House School Division, Department 9106, 400 Hahn Rd, Westminster, MD 21157) is "a comprehensive developmental language-arts program that incorporates the teaching of composition, vocabulary, grammar, usage, and study skills with creative and functional writing tasks" (p. 4). It can be used in the elementary or secondary grades. Components include 12 worktexts (96 pages each) at three levels of difficulty. At each level, worktexts focus on composition, grammar and usage, study skills, and vocabulary. Each is accompanied by a teacher's edition. Pretests and posttests accompany each text. A teacher's guide for the program is also available.

The first English, Inc. course is designed to teach third- and fourth-grade level skills with the vocabulary used not exceeding the fourth-grade level. The second course is designed to teach fifth- and sixth-grade level skills with the vocabulary used not exceeding the sixth-grade level. The third course is designed to teach seventh- and eighth-grade level skills with the vocabulary used not exceeding the eighth-grade level. Difficulty of the passages was controlled with the Fry readability formula (Fry, 1977) and through use of The Living Word Vocabulary (Dale & O'Rourke, 1976).

The program can be used in two ways. First, one skill area can be focused on by having students complete all the lessons in one book and at all levels, if appropriate. Second, the books can be integrated so that all four books at one level are used together. The teacher's guide suggests that, in either case, instruction should begin in a composition book. The student is therefore prepared to complete "Writer at Work" activities in the other books.

Students are placed in the program according to the results obtained from pretests. Initial tests are selected by using the students' reading levels and perceived skills levels. The pretests take approx-imately 20 minutes to administer. Each book is also accompanied by a posttest.

Skills emphasized in the texts include the following:

- Composition (writing sentences and paragraphs; different styles of writing; individual letters; and the mechanics of capitalization, punctuation, and editing),
- Vocabulary (understanding prefixes/suffixes and antonyms/synonyms; understanding word meanings; and being able to use words as idioms and metaphors);
- Grammar and usage (focusing on nouns, pronouns, verbs, adjectives, adverbs, prepositions, sentences, and usage);
- Study skills (focusing on how to use a dictionary, going to the library; book parts, including references; organizing a report; reading tables, graphs, and maps; and test taking).

Each text contains an introduction to the book which discusses the importance of the skill. Each text also contains an editing checklist, which contains questions about sentences/paragraphs and capitalization/punctuation rules. A lesson about the checklist appears in each composition book. Students are encouraged to use the list throughout the program. The vocabulary books contain glossaries that list words unknown by 80% of fourth, sixth, and eighth graders according to the Living Word Vocabulary (Dale & O'Rourke, 1976). The glossary also includes prefixes, suffixes, roots, and vocabulary terms taught in the book.

Lessons in the texts (1–4 pages) follow a similar format. Lessons begin with instruction in a specific skill and "rules," which are set off in boxes. Exercises in the skill follow: "Practice exercises are not presented in standardized formats that promote rigid and mechanical responses, but are deliberately varied. Some are made nonobjective in order to give students a chance to read directions, *think,* and give answers that reflect their own lives" (teacher's guide, p. 9). Many lessons end with a "Writer at Work" activity (application). Sometimes, tips are presented in the margins for students to use in writing. Review pages appear at the end of each unit of instruction. Texts are illustrated occasionally with line drawings that, in many cases, are cartoon-like.

The teacher's editions contain objectives for each lesson, notes for enhancing the lesson (e.g., by combining it with pages from one of the other books), and answers. In addition, some suggestions are provided for grading the "Writer at Work" activity.

The teacher's guide gives an overview of the program, a list of skills taught in each text, suggestions for teaching the program, suggestions for grading, and follow-up activities for units of instruction.

English, Inc.—in particular the composition books—is an excellent program for students in the intermediate and secondary grades experiencing difficulties in writing. As its full name implies, the focus is on effective *writing*. Students are given ample opportunities to write using activities that are varied and interesting.

Two somewhat negative points in the program are easily corrected. First, the pre- and posttests are not very useful because they test a limited number of the skills taught in the program, so the best way to determine placement is to use the teacher's knowledge of students' reading and skill levels. Second, the guide suggests beginning with the composition books; however, for students who cannot yet write complete sentences, it may be better to begin instruction with the sentences pages in the grammar and usage text. As research has indicated, there would be little value in having students complete the parts of speech lessons. Our review would suggest that the vocabulary and study skills texts are of little direct value for improving composition skills.

Writing for a Reason Course

The Writing for a Reason Course (Alzofon, Bledsoe, Costantini, Kelly, Orina, Rhodes, Rogoff, & Scott, 1985; available from Quercus Corporation, 2405 Castro Valley Blvd, Castro Valley, CA 94546) is designed to provide a foundation upon which below grade level students in grades 7–12 may improve their writing skills.

The program is broken up into various components. Writing for a Reason includes five books, each accompanied by a complimentary teachers' guide. The four books of More Writing Practice accompany the first four books of Writing for a Reason. Audio Tape for Writing for a Reason-5 Grammar for Sentences consists of two books, each accompanied by a complimentary teachers' guide.

Each Writing for a Reason text focuses on a specific set of skills. Writing for a Reason-1 teaches students to write simple sentences, notes or messages, directions to a place, and directions for how to do something. Also taught are rules for capitalization (beginning of a sentence, names of people and streets) and punctuation (period at end of sentence and abbreviation, apostrophe in contractions).

Writing for a Reason-2 focuses on writing invitations, addressing envelopes, writing letters to answer invitations, filling out job applications, and writing business letters. Also taught are rules for capitalization (names of days, months, states, and cities) and for writing times and dates (using a colon and commas). A list of two-letter abbreviations for the 50 states is given.

Writing for a Reason-3 teaches the parts of a standard paragraph, how to write a descriptive paragraph, when to change paragraphs, and how to write and punctuate conversation. Punctuation rules taught include quotation marks for a quote, using a comma before a quote, and using commas to separate words in a list.

Writing for a Reason-4 teaches the use of adjectives, adverbs, and similies and how to write a narrative, a comparison, and a persuasive argument. Writing for a Reason-5 teaches students how to listen (focusing on main ideas and details) and take notes in outline form and how to write announcements and news articles.

The texts contain explanations for all activities, which students read before writing. The readability of all texts is second-grade level to allow students to proceed independently. Rules (or tips) for writing and/or listening are enclosed in boxes for emphasis. Nice features of the first three texts are lists of rules to remember that appear on the last page, which could serve as handy references for students. Numerous specific examples are provided for each skill, and students then practice the skill. Some black-and-white illustrations are provided to stimulate interest. The audiotape for the fifth text is designed to stimulate interest by focusing on news features presented by a fictitious radio station.

The More Writing Practice (MWP) books each contain 21 pages of additional exercises and are used concurrently with the Writing for a Reason texts. Students are directed to specific MWP pages by the Writing for a Reason text.

The teachers' guides for Writing for a Reason texts are brief (four pages each for texts 1–4) and contain a brief overview of the program with brief suggestions for extension activities, along with answer keys. The guide for the fifth text contains transcripts for the audiotape. In addition, in texts 1–4 a posttest is provided that can be duplicated to assess the students' knowledge of skills taught upon completion of each text.

The Grammar for Sentences texts are write-in texts. They are written at a second-grade reading level (according to the Spache formula) and are similar in format to the Writing for a Reason texts. Grammar for Sentences-1 emphasizes using adjectives, adverbs, compound subjects or verbs, objects, prepositions, and subject–verb agreement. Grammar for Sentences-2 teaches the student to write compound and complex sentences through instruction in conjunctions and clauses. The second text seems to be appropriate for use after Writing for a Reason-1.

Writing for a Reason, More Writing Practice, and Grammar for Sentences-2 provide a good foundation for teaching writing skills to upper-grade-level students. The series is sold for students in grades 7–12 but appears useful for students in grades 5 and above. The books are written at a low reading level so that students with poor reading skills can benefit from the program. The implication in the teachers' guides is that students can proceed on an independent basis; however, it would seem more appropriate to provide more teacher guidance. As the authors point out, although the texts are designed as a series, they can be used separately to meet specific students' needs.

Writing Sentences, Paragraphs, and Compositions

Writing Sentences, Paragraphs, and Compositions (Granowsky & Dawkins, 1986; available from Modern Curriculum Press, 13900 Prospect Rd, Cleveland, OH 44136) is "designed to allow students to practice basic writing skills and to derive satisfaction from putting their thoughts down clearly on paper." Components of the program include five 96-page workbooks: levels B–F or reading levels grade 2–6.

Activities in the beginning of each book (about half of book B and about one fourth of books C–F) focus on writing sentences. Examples of specific skills include writing complete sentences, details in sentences, writing questions and exclamations, combining sentences, combining subjects and predicates, adding phrases to sentences, and writing appositives.

The second and third sections of each book provide instruction and practice in writing paragraphs and compositions. Examples of specific skills covered include using main idea sentences; describing a person, thing, setting, or character; writing notes or letters; writing to explain; writing a science report; writing a book report; and writing a poem, story, or tall tale.

Lessons begin with an instruction section that explains the skill being practiced and often provides a sample. In book B, lessons for sentences are divided into sections called "Learn" (instruction), "Practice," "Your Turn" (more extensive writing), and "Check." Lessons for paragraph and composition writing are divided into five sections: "Sample" (explanation and sample), "Practice" (practice with little or no creative writing), "Plan" (a prewriting experience to help students select topics, organize thoughts, write a topic sentence, organize an outline, and fill in the details), "First Draft" (write, rewrite, edit, and proofread), and "Final Edition." The final edition section is followed by a teacher's comments section that includes a box where the teacher can indicate whether certain items are good or need work. An answer key appears in the back of each book. All book pages are perforated.

Lessons are usually illustrated with black-and-white photographs. Topics for writing are varied and interesting (e.g., a favorite place, pets, sports, etc.). Sample paragraphs also cover a variety of topics.

Books C–F include six pretest (or posttest) pages assessing capitalization, punctuation, and usage skills. Items are keyed to lessons in other books in the MCP Writing Mastery Program, including Mastering Capitalization, Mastering Punctuation, and Mastering Usage (all available from Modern Curriculum Press). The teacher can also use these books if he or she notices a student needs practice in a specific skill when grading the final edition. A skills index for the books is printed on the inside back cover.

Writing Sentences, Paragraphs, and Compositions is an excellent series for students experiencing difficulties in written composition. Although implied use is at the reading level grade, the series can be used with older students because the content should appeal to students of a variety of ages. Students are provided with instructional/sample sections and are given ample opportunity to write. The students are taught the processes of writing, continuing what has been stressed in the instructional program.

Writer's Handbook and Handbook E for Young Writers

Writer's Handbook and Handbook E for Young Writers (Cranford, Goodman, Lewis, & Pletz, 1982, 1985; available from J. B. Harber Publishing, PO Box 96146, Houston, TX 77213) are reference texts we have found useful for student use. The former is geared for students in grades 7 and up. The latter incorporates skills commonly taught through grade 5. Both books include sections that define paragraphs and types of writing, give examples of linking words, describe good sentence writing, list capitalization and punctuation rules, etc.

SUMMARY

A consistent theme throughout this chapter is that students learn to write by writing. Students must write every day—particularly writing that requires them to use all stages of the writing process: planning, writing, and revising. In addition to specific instruction in composition, students need formal instruction in handwriting and spelling. The other mechanics of writing (e.g., capitalization and punctuation) should be taught in response to a student's needs as indicated by his or her writing. Well-designed commercial programs are available in all of these areas.

Appendix A: Reviews of Norm-Referenced Tests

CRITERIA FOR TEST REVIEWS

Standardization

If a test is well standardized, the demographic data for the sample should be similar to the United States census data in terms of sex, race, socioeconomic level, geographic distribution, and urban/rural residence. Further, there should be approximately 100 subjects per age or grade level.

Reliability

Ideally, test–retest data should be provided by age or grade level, and correlations should be .85 or higher with a 2-week retest interval. Internal consistency coefficients of the same magnitude would be acceptable. Interrater reliability should be at least .80 or higher. Standard errors of measurement should be provided by age or grade level.

Validity

To specify criteria for validity is difficult because of the complexity of the issues involved. A good test manual should provide a clear description of the rationale for item selection to assure examiners of the content validity of a test. Information should be provided on item analyses, criterion-related validity, and construct validity.

To assist in evaluating the content validity of spelling tests, the Fitzgerald (1951) list of high-frequency words was used as a reference. Discussion of the rational for use of this list is provided in Chapter 5.

BASIC ACHIEVEMENT SKILLS INDIVIDUAL SCREENER

General Description

The Basic Achievement Skills Individual Screener (BASIS, 1983; available from Psychological Corporation, 555 Academic Court, San Antonio, TX 78204-0952) was written for use with students in grades 1 through post–high school. The written expression skill tested is spelling, and an optional sample of spontaneous writing is included. Reading and Mathematics subtests are also included in the BASIS. Individual administration is suggested. The spelling test is not timed; students are given 10 minutes to complete the optional spontaneous writing exercise.

There is one form of the test. A basal level is defined as meeting the criterion for a grade-level cluster of spelling words, and the discontinue level is where this criterion is not met. Scores can be reported in terms of standard scores (mean of 100, standard deviation of 15), percentile ranks, stanines, or age or grade equivalents. Test materials for the writing sections consist of the examiner's manual and the protocol.

Description of Spelling and Writing Sections

Spelling

Words for this subtest are presented in clusters of six for grade levels 1 through 8. The student is required to write each word from dictation.

Writing

This optional subtest is for use with students in grades 3–8. The student is asked to write for a 10-minute period on the topic "My Favorite Place." This writing sample is compared with a sample selected from samples obtained from a group of students whose writing was evaluated using the holistic scoring method. If such a comparison cannot be made, the sample can be evaluated informally in terms of ideas, organization, vocabulary, sentence structure, and mechanics. No score is given for this subtest. Criteria for evaluation are general and vague.

Technical Adequacy

Standardization

There were more than 100 students per grade level in the sample, which, for the most part, corresponded to 1970 U.S. census data; the sample was similar in terms of sex, geographic region, and race, but ethnicity was not addressed. There were too many children included from low socioeconomic levels. Students were selected to correspond to school system size rather than on the basis of urban/rural residence.

Reliability

Test–retest. A 2- to 4-week retest interval was used. Correlations for the Spelling subtest were .95 ($n = 60$) for grade 2; .89 ($n = 66$) for grade 5; and .89 ($n = 52$) for grade 8. Data were not given for other grade levels.

Internal consistency. For the Spelling subtest, correlations ranged from .87 to .96 across grade levels.

Interrater. For the spontaneous writing section, untrained raters scored papers and obtained an interrater agreement of almost two-thirds (p. 146). This is very low agreement; the usual criterion for acceptable interrater reliability is at least 80%.

Standard errors of measurement. Information is provided by either grade or age level.

Validity

Content. Spelling items were selected from the 1978 Metropolitan Achievement Tests (developed from review of nine spelling series for grades 1–4 and seven series for grades 5–8). Criteria for selecting words from this list are described in the manual. The reading level of the words is at least one grade level below the level of the tested items. There are six items per grade level for a total of 48 words. A comparison of these words with the Fitzgerald list of words used frequently in writing indicates that 58% of the words are high-frequency words. Specific comparisons by grade level revealed the following: grade 1, 83%; grade 2, 66%; grade 3, 100%; grade 4, 83%; grade 5, 50%; grade 6, 50%; grade 7, 33%; grade 8, 0%.

Because no specific criteria are given for scoring the writing subtest, it is difficult to obtain useful information from this section.

Criterion-related. No information is provided for the subtests involving writing.

Construct. Not addressed.

Conclusions

Given the validity problems with the writing subtests (i.e., the percentage of high-frequency words for Spelling for grades 5 and up and the subjective evaluation of Writing), the BASIS cannot be recommended for use in making eligibility decisions, nor would it provide a sufficient sample of educationally important skills for planning programs. In terms of technical adequacy, the standardization was quite representative, except for problems with socioeconomic level. Test–retest data were good for Spelling but were provided only for three grade levels. Information on criterion-related and construct validity are lacking.

BASIC SCHOOL SKILLS INVENTORY–DIAGNOSTIC

General Description

The Basic School Skills Inventory-Diagnostic (BSSI-D, 1976, 1983; written by Donald Hammill and James Leigh, and available from PRO-ED, 8700 Shoal Creek Blvd., Austin, TX 78758) was designed for use with children 4-0 to 6-11. On the Writing subtest, a variety of written expression skills are assessed. The test also has Daily Living Skills, Spoken Language, Reading, Mathematics, and Classroom Behavior subtests. Administration time for the entire inventory is about 30 minutes, and it is completed on an individual basis. The BSSI-D was designed to be completed by someone, such as the classroom teacher, who has observed the student's performance in the classroom over time. Thus, items can be scored based on this knowledge or from direct administration of some items. The Writing subtest requires considerably less than 30 minutes to complete. There is one form of the test. For the Writing subtest, a basal is defined as five consecutive correct items and a ceiling as three items missed in a row. Scores can be reported in terms of percentiles or standard scores (mean of 10, standard deviation of 3) for the subtests. Materials needed for the Writing subtest include the examiner's manual, a protocol, a pencil for the student, lined paper, a card containing a common word, and a chalkboard.

Description of the Writing Subtest

There are 15 items assessing skills needed for writing letters, words and sentences (see p. 7 of the BSSI-D). A student can use manuscript or cursive writing. Examples of the various writing skills tested are writing letters, copying words and sentences from a card and the chalkboard, spelling, use of capitalization and punctuation rules, writing syntactically correct sentences, and composing a story.

Technical Adequacy

Standardization

Though 376 children were included in the standardization, the number per age level is not given. Fifty-one percent of the children were boys. In comparison to the U.S. census data, the sample was low on children from the East and high on children from the South and North Central regions. The sample description did not address ethnicity and had about half the number of black children needed. There were too many rural children and too many children from blue collar families.

Reliability

Test–retest.   No data are provided.

Internal consistency.   For the Writing subtest, coefficients were as follows: .87 for age 4; .89 for age 5; and .87 for age 6.

Standard errors of measurement.   Data are given for each age level.

Validity

Content.   Items were selected based on (1) input from teachers regarding skills that seemed to discriminate between children "ready" for school and those who were not; (2) results of several field tests; and (3) the use of item analysis.

Criterion-related.   Results of the Writing subtest correlated .22 with teacher ratings of readiness.

Construct.   Scores were shown to increase with age; subtests were found to correlate well with each other; children labeled LD were found to score lower on the BSSI-D than non-LD students. Also, the discriminating power of the items was examined in the item analysis: For the Writing subtest, results were .10 at age 4; .48 at age 5; and .50 at age 6. Thus, at age 4 items did not have good discriminating power on this subtest.

Conclusions

Though the Writing subtest on the BSSI-D might provide some general screening information about a child's progress in written expression, it is unlikely that children aged 4–6 would qualify for special education services as LD due to problems in written expression. It seems that any difficulties noted in this area could be handled in the regular classroom because of the limited number of skills that would be involved. In terms of technical adequacy, there are problems with the representativeness of the sample, no test–retest data are given, data on criterion-related validity are needed, and the discriminating power of items for age 4 is weak. Further, given the ceiling rules and the limited number of items on the subtest, results are likely to based on a rather small sample of written expression skills. Use of this subtest is not likely to provide much useful information.

DIAGNOSTIC ACHIEVEMENT BATTERY

General Description

The Diagnostic Achievement Battery (DAB, 1984; written by Phyllis Newcomer and Dolores Curtis, and available from PRO-ED, 8700 Shoal Creek Blvd, Austin, TX 78758) was designed for students aged 6-0 to 14-11. For written expression, the test covers capitalization, punctuation, spelling, and vocabulary. The test also contains subtests that assess listening, speaking, reading, and mathematics skills. Any or all of the subtests can be given. The DAB is individually administered. For the Capitalization and Punctuation subtest, there is a 15-minute time limit; Written Vocabulary also has a 15-minute time limit, but the Spelling subtest is not timed. There is one form of the test. No basal or ceiling rules are used for Capitalization and Punctuation or Written Vocabulary. Spelling begins with item #1 and testing is discontinued when five items in a row are missed. Results can be reported in terms of standard scores (for subtests, mean is 10, standard deviation is 3; for composites, mean is 100, standard deviation is 15) or percentiles. Test materials consist of an examiner's manual, a protocol, and a student worksheet.

Description of Subtests

Capitalization and Punctuation

A student is required to provide capitalization and punctuation in a printed paragraph that contains no capitalization or punctuation marks. For capitalization, the following rules are assessed (numbers indicate the number of items per rule):

- Beginning of sentences (12)
- Names of people (9, plus 2 that also appear at the beginning of sentences and one that is the first word of a quotation)
- Pronoun "I" (1)
- Streets (2)
- Cities (2), states (2), province (1), countries (4)
- Day of the week (1), months (2)
- Businesses (3)

For punctuation, the following marks are assessed:

- Period (12 at ends of sentences and 2 for abbreviations)
- Comma (1 series, 1 preceding date, 1 following date, 1 separating city and state, 1 separating province and country, 1 for a nonrestrictive clause, 4 for appositives, 1 after name in direct address, and 1 separating speaker and quotation)
- Quotation mark (1)
- Apostrophe (2 contractions, 1 possessive)

Spelling

A student is asked to write up to 20 words dictated by the examiner.

Written Vocabulary

This subtest requires that the student write a story based on three pictures representing a version of the fable "The Tortoise and the Hare." Maturity of vocabulary is evaluated by counting the number of seven-letter words used by the student.

Technical Adequacy

Standardization

The number of students per age level is not given. The demographic characteristics of the sample correspond closely to 1980 U.S. census data in terms of sex, geographic area, race, socioeconomic level as defined by parental occupation, and urban/rural residence. Ethnicity is not addressed.

Reliability

Test–retest. Data are provided for 34 students who were 9-11 to 13-3. A 2-week retest interval was employed. Correlations for written expression subtests were as follows: Capitalization, .93; Punctuation, .95; Spelling, .96; and Written Vocabulary, .83. The Written Language Composite Correlation (made up of results from these four subtests) was .99. No data are given for other age levels.

Internal consistency. The formats for Capitalization, Punctuation, and Written Vocabulary were not appropriate for use with coefficient alpha. Correlations for the Spelling subtest were .93, ages 6 and 7; .84, ages 8 and 9; and .83, age 11.

Standard errors of measurement. Data are given for all subtests and composites.

Validity

Content. The authors reviewed common curricula to develop items; the specific curricula reviewed were not indicated. Item analysis was employed to select items.

For the Capitalization and Punctuation subtests, no readability information is presented for the material, which may be too difficult for first graders and beginning second graders. Examiners should check to see that students are able to read material where they miss items. The print for this subtest is small and leaves little room for students to write responses; this may be frustrating for some students. Items are not keyed to the rules tested. For Capitalization, a number of items require knowledge of the rule to capitalize names of people, and for Punctuation, many items require use of a period at the end of sentences; because of this, at several age levels students could score within the average range with knowledge of only one rule.

On the Spelling subtest, only 9 of the 20 words appear on the

Fitzgerald list of high-frequency words. These 9 words appear in the first 11 words tested.

For the Written Vocabulary subtest, further research would be helpful to determine whether use of words with "seven or more letters" is an adequate definition for mature vocabulary.

Criterion-related. Research with 25 third graders and 21 sixth graders indicated that the Capitalization subtest correlated .41 with the Style subtest of the Test of Written Language (TOWL). The Punctuation subtest correlated .47 with the Style subtest of the TOWL. Spelling correlated .81 with the TOWL Spelling subtest. Written Vocabulary correlated .37 with the Vocabulary subtest of the TOWL. The Written Language Quotient of the DAB correlated .64 with the results of the Style, Spelling, and Vocabulary subtests of the TOWL.

Construct. Results of the DAB subtests for written expression were found to correlate with age and grade (.41 to .74), correlated well with other subtests (.33 to .83), and correlated with results of the Slossen and the Otis-Lennon IQ tests (.36 to .59). Further, significant differences were found between LD and non-LD students on the DAB. However, IQ differences were not controlled in this study.

Conclusions

The standardization for the DAB appears to correspond to U.S. census data on important demographic characteristics, and test–retest data are adequate for ages 9-11 to 13-3. However, further test–retest data are needed for other age levels and should be given by age level. Because of the problems noted with the content validity of the subtests for written expression, this test cannot be recommended for use in making eligibility decisions. However, the Written Vocabulary subtest might provide useful information for this aspect of written expression.

DIAGNOSTIC ACHIEVEMENT TEST FOR ADOLESCENTS

General Description

The Diagnostic Achievement Test for Adolescents (DATA, 1986; written by Phyllis Newcomer and Brian Bryant, and available from PRO-ED, 8700 Shoal Creek Blvd, Austin, TX 78758) can be used with students aged 12-0 to 18-11. Written expression skills tested include spelling and level of vocabulary used in writing. The test also includes subtests for reading, math, science, social studies, and reference skills. The entire test requires 1–2 hours to administer and is given individually. There is one form of the test. For the Spelling subtest, the basal is five consecutive correct items, and the ceiling is three consecutive errors. Results can be reported in terms of standard scores (mean of 10, standard deviation of 3 for subtests; mean of 100, standard deviation of 15 for composites) or percentiles. Test materials needed for the written expression sections are the examiner's manual, a protocol, the student booklet, and a student response form.

Description of Subtests

Spelling

For this subtest, the student is asked to write up to 45 words dictated by the examiner.

Writing Composition

The student is asked to write a story based on three black-and-white pictures. The story is scored for the number of words with seven or more letters.

Technical Adequacy

Standardization

The sample included over 100 students at each age level, except for age 18 where there were 97. The demographic characteristics of the sample closely corresponded to the 1985 U.S. census data in terms of sex, geographic distribution, race, ethnicity, and urban/rural residence. No information is included on the socioeconomic level of the sample.

Reliability

Test–retest. A 1-week retest interval was used with 58 students 12 through 18 years of age. The correlation for the Spelling subtest was .95; for Writing Composition .71, and for the Writing Composite (based on results of Spelling plus Writing Composition) .88.

Internal consistency. Correlations for the Spelling subtest were .95 for ages 12–13; .97 for ages 14–15; and .97 for ages 16–18. The

Writing Composition format was not appropriate for use with coefficient alpha.

Standard errors of measurement. Data are provided for three age groups: 12–13, 14–15, and 16–18.

Validity

Content. Items were selected for the Spelling subtest from the EDL Core Vocabularies in Reading, Mathematics, Science, and Social Studies. Items were selected from this item pool based on item analysis. Only 1 of the 45 spelling words appears on the Fitzgerald list of high-frequency words. Also, whether use of words with seven or more letters is an adequate measure of mature vocabulary remains to be demonstrated by further research.

Criterion-related. Correlations with the Iowa Test of Basic Skills (ITBS) were as follows: ITBS Spelling and DATA Spelling, $r = .66$; ITBS Total Language and DATA Writing Composition, $r = .42$; ITBS Total Language and DATA Writing Composite, $r = .54$.

Construct. Scores were shown to increase with age; subtests were shown to correlate with each other; scores were shown to correlate with the Short Form Test of Academic Achievement; and 34 LD children were shown to score significantly different from non-LD students. Discriminating powers for items on the Spelling subtest ranged from .56 to .72.

Conclusions

It is unfortunate that so few of the spelling words on the DATA are high-frequency words. Because there are other norm-referenced tests that are reasonably technically adequate, and that are made up of a substantial number of high-frequency words, the DATA is not the best choice to measure spelling. The test–retest correlation was too low for the Writing Composition subtest, and only a 1-week interval was employed. Though the standardization appears representative (except for the lack of information on socioeconomic levels), and the Writing Composite has adequate reliability, other technically adequate measures would seem to be better choices than the DATA because they do not have some of the limitations noted above in terms of validity.

DIAGNOSTIC SPELLING POTENTIAL TEST

General Description

The Diagnostic Spelling Potential Test (DSPT, 1982; written by John Arena, and available from Academic Therapy Publications, 20 Commercial Blvd, Novato, CA 94947) was designed for ages 7-0 to adult. The manual suggests that it be given individually. Administration time varies from 25 to 40 minutes. There are two forms of the test (A and B). A basal is defined as five consecutive correct responses and a ceiling as five consecutive errors for the Spelling and Word Recognition subtests. The Visual Recognition and Auditory–Visual Recognition subtests have a ceiling of six errors within eight responses. Results can be reported in terms of standard scores (mean or 100, standard deviation of 15), percentiles, or grade ratings. Test materials include an examiner's manual and a protocol.

Description of Subtests

Spelling

Each form consists of 90 words dictated by the examiner.

Word Recognition

This subtest taps decoding skills. There are 90 items per form. A student is asked to read each word. If a response is delayed for 2 seconds or more, or the student self-corrects, then the response is coded as use of phonetic decoding. If a word is recognized in less than 2 seconds, it is coded as a sight vocabulary word.

Visual Recognition

These 90 items tap recognition of the correct spelling of words. There are four choices given for each word.

Auditory–Visual Recognition

The same 90 items are used as for the Visual Recognition subtest. However, for this subtest the examiner says the word and uses it in a sentence. The student is asked to circle the correct spelling.

Technical Adequacy

Standardization

Only 611 students from grades 1 through 12 were included in the sample. Data were collected partially through group administration of the DSPT and partially through individual administration. All students were from the San Francisco Bay area. No other data are provided. Hence, the normative group did not consist of a nationally representative group of students.

Reliability

Test–retest. No data are given.

Alternate form. For the Spelling subtest, the following correlations were obtained: primary grades, .95; for the elementary levels, .95; and for the secondary levels, .91.

Standard errors of measurement. Information is given in terms of primary, elementary, and secondary levels for each subtest.

Validity

Content. The only information given for this area is that the words were selected initially from the 1954 New Iowa Spelling Scale and the 1953 New Standard High School Spelling Scale. Additional words were selected from unspecified sources to ensure an adequate ceiling. However, less than half of the words on Form A (39 of 90) and on Form B (42 of 90) are high-frequency words according to the Fitzgerald list.

Criterion-related. Average correlations (for Forms A and B) with the 1978 Wide Range Achievement Test were as follows: primary grades, .92; elementary grades, .93; and secondary grades, .89.

Diagnostic. The mean score for Spelling (73.08) for 25 secondary students who were in a school for "the learning handicapped" was significantly lower than the mean of 100 for the test.

Conclusions

Because of the unrepresentativeness of the sample, the lack of test–retest data, and problems with content validity, the DSPT cannot be recommended.

KAUFMAN TEST OF EDUCATIONAL ACHIEVEMENT

General Description

The Kaufman Test of Educational Achievement (KTEA, 1985; written by Allen Kaufman and Nadine Kaufman, and available from American Guidance Service, Publishers' Building, Circle Pines, MN 55014-1796) is for use with students in grades 1 through 12. Spelling is the written expression skill included on the KTEA; subtests for reading and mathematics are also included on the scale. The test is given individually, and the entire test takes from 30 to 90 minutes. There is one form of the KTEA.

Items are grouped in units. Basals are defined in terms of two items passed in one unit or by returning to the first item. A ceiling occurs when a student fails all items within a unit. Results are reported in terms of standard scores with a mean of 100 and a standard deviation of 15. Materials for the Spelling subtest consist of an examiner's manual, a protocol, and a spelling sheet.

Description of the Spelling Subtest

This subtest consists of 50 items. The protocol is arranged to allow for analysis of errors with "word parts"—that is prefixes and word beginnings, suffixes and word endings, closed-syllable vowels, open-syllable and final "e" pattern vowels, vowel digraphs and diphthongs, "r"-controlled patterns, consonant clusters and digraphs, and single and double consonants. "Whole-word" errors can also be noted.

Technical Adequacy

Standardization

There are two sets of norm tables. Data for the spring norms are based on more than 100 students per grade level. Data for the fall norms are based on more than 80 students per grade level. The sample closely approximates the 1980 U.S. census in terms of sex, geographic distribution, socioeconomic level as defined by parental education, race, and ethnicity. Urban/rural residence is not addressed.

Reliability

Test–retest. The data are based on the performance of 172 students in grades 1 through 12. The retest interval varied from 1 to 35 days, and data were grouped for grades 1 through 6 and grades 7 through 12; this retest interval and grouping of data could have resulted in inflated correlation coefficients. If data had been provided by grade level with a 2-week interval, this information would have been more useful. The correlation for the Spelling subtest for grades 1 through 6 was .95 and for grades 7 through 12 was .96.

Internal consistency. For the Spelling subtest, correlations for all grade levels exceeded .85.

Standard errors of measurement. This information is provided by both age and grade level.

Validity

Content. An item pool was developed from review of several spelling series, and items were reviewed by experts. Item analysis was used in the final item selection. Of the 50 words, 27 (54%) appear on the Fitzgerald list of high-frequency words; these include the first 23 words. The Spelling subtest may not be useful with first graders because a raw score as low as 2 falls within the average range. The error analysis is not very useful because words are not separated into rule-governed and non-rule-governed categories, and there are too few items with which to look at error patterns with specific elements.

Criterion-related. Correlations of the Spelling subtest of the KTEA and other spelling measures were as follows: Wide Range Achievement Test Spelling, .50 to .90; Peabody Individual Achievement Test Spelling, .78.

Construct. Scores were shown to increase with age and to correlate highly with the composite score. Correlations of the Spelling subtest results with other measures of achievement were as follows: .14 to .88 with the Kaufman Achievement Battery for Children (KABC); .29 to .51 with the Peabody Picture Vocabulary Test-Revised (PPVT-R); .52 to .68 with the Stanford, .49 to .69 with the Metropolitan Achievement Test; and .45 to .65 with the Comprehensive Test of Basic Skills.

Conclusions

The KTEA Spelling subtest could provide useful norm-referenced scores for students in grades 2 through 8. For upper level grades, students are not asked to spell high-frequency words. In terms of technical adequacy, the standardization is very good, as are the data on reliability. However, additional data by grade level are needed for test–retest reliability. The validity of the items appears to be good through about the eighth-grade level.

PEABODY INDIVIDUAL ACHIEVEMENT TEST

General Description

The Peabody Individual Achievement Test (PIAT, 1970; written by Lloyd Dunn and Frederick Markwardt, and available American Guidance Service, Publishers' Building, Circle Pines, MN 55014) is designed for use with students in grades K through 12. The written expression skill assessed is spelling; subtests for reading and math are also included in the test. The PIAT is individually administered and requires 30–40 minutes for the entire test. There is one form of the PIAT. A basal is defined as five consecutive correct responses and a ceiling as five errors within seven responses. Results can be expressed in terms of grade or age equivalents, percentiles, or standard scores (mean of 100, standard deviation of 15). Test materials needed for the Spelling subtest include the examiner's manual, the easel book of items, and the protocol.

Description of the Spelling Subtest

The 84 items on this subtest include distinguishing letters from pictures and numbers, finding letters by their names, and recognizing words given by the examiner. For each item, the student must choose the correct answer from four alternatives; no writing of words is involved.

Technical Adequacy

Standardization

More than 100 students were included at each grade level in the sample. The demographic characteristics of the sample closely approximated the 1967 U.S. census data in terms of sex, geographic distribution, race, occupational level, and urban/rural residence. Ethnicity was not addressed.

Reliability

Test–retest. A 1-month retest interval was used with students in grades K, 1, 3, 5, 8, and 12. Correlations for the Spelling subtest were all less than .85.

Internal consistency. No information was given because split-half reliability techniques were felt to be inappropriate for a test with items ordered in terms of difficulty and where basals and ceilings were used.

Standard errors of measurement. Information is provided for each grade level.

Validity

Content. Words for the Spelling subtest were selected from a review of written language tests, the Buckingham Extension of the Ayres Spelling Scale, the List of Spelling Difficulties in 3,876 Words, the New Iowa Spelling Scale, and the New Standard High School Spelling Scale. The Furness list of commonly misspelled words, dictionaries, and magazines were also reviewed. This resulted in a pool of 1,000 words from which the items were selected after item analysis when words were administered in a dictated format.

The multiple-choice format of this subtest allows guessing to influence results. Also, because of the format, a student who is good at word recognition, but poor at spelling, could be identified as a good speller on this subtest. The percentage of words that appear on the Fitzgerald high-frequency word list is only 39%.

Criterion-related. Results correlated with results of the Peabody Picture Vocabulary Test at .57 and of the Wide Range Achievement Test Spelling at .85.

Construct. This was not addressed.

Conclusions

Given the problems with validity due to the multiple-choice format and the words tested, the Spelling subtest cannot be recommended. Further, the standardization is out of date, and the reliability is poor.

QUICK SCORE ACHIEVEMENT TEST

General Description

The Quick Score Achievement Test (QSAT, 1987; written by Donald Hammill, Jerome Ammer, Mary Cronin, Linda Mandlebaum, and Sally Quinby, and is available from PRO-ED, 8700 Shoal Creek Blvd, Austin, TX 78758) is for use with students aged 7-0 to 17-11. For written expression, the test assesses capitalization, punctuation, and spelling. The QSAT also includes sections for testing reading, arithmetic, and knowledge of facts. Administration is individual and requires about 10–20 minutes for the Writing subtest. There are two forms (A and B) of the test. The Writing subtest begins with item 1 and continues until a ceiling of five consecutive failures is met. Results can be reported in terms of percentiles or standard scores (mean of 10, standard deviation of 3). Testing materials consist of an examiner's manual, a student record form, and a profile sheet.

Description of the Writing Subtest

A student is asked to write graded sentences dictated by the examiner. Each form is made up of 22 sentences. Each sentence requires use of a form of punctuation or capitalization and the spelling of a word taught at the grade level tested. Memory skills are not likely to confound results because a sentence can be repeated up to four times.

The following capitalization skills are tested:

	Form A	Form B
Beginning of sentences	22	22
Names of people	5 (However, these also appear at the beginning of sentences.)	8 (plus 5 that also appear at the beginning of sentences)
Pronoun "I"	3	4
Name of country	0	1
Body of water	1	0
Day of the week	1	0
Month	1	0
Titles of people	2	2
Title of publication	1	0
Special group	0	1

	Form A	Form B
First word in quotation	3	1
Proper adjective	0	1
Letter grade	0	1

Punctuation skills tested include:

Form A	Form B
Period. 20 at ends of sentences, 2 abbreviations	20 at ends of sentences, 2 abbreviations
Question mark. 2	2
Comma. 1 in a date, 2 words in series, 1 after introductory word, 3 separating speaker and quotation, 3 for non-restrictive clause, 3 appositives	2 for words in series, 1 after introductory word, 2 separating speaker and quotation, 3 for nonrestrictive clause, 3 for appositives, 1 after name in direct address
Quotation marks. 2	2
Apostrophe. 2 for contractions, 1 for plural number, 2 for plural letters, 1 for possessive	1 for a contraction, 1 for a plural letter, 1 for a possessive
Colon. 2 for time	1 for introducing a list
Semicolon. 1 for compound sentence	1 in series with commas
Underlining. 1 for book	0
Hyphen. 0	1

A large percentage of the words in the sentences are high-frequency words according to the Fitzgerald list: on Form A, 66% of the different words are high frequency; on Form B, 68% of the different words are high-frequency words.

Technical Adequacy

Standardization

There were more than 100 subjects per age level in the sample. Demographic data were similar to 1985 U.S. census data in terms of sex, geographic distribution, race, ethnicity, and urban/rural residence. No data are presented for socioeconomic level.

Reliability

Test–retest. A correlation of .83 was obtained for the Writing subtest with an interval of 1 day to 2 weeks ($n = 115$). Data are not given by age level.

Internal consistency. Of the 10 coefficients for Writing, 8 were above .85.

Standard errors of measurement. Information is given for each subtest.

Validity

Content. Items for capitalization and punctuation were selected based on review of cited sources and cited curriculum materials to ensure that items were educationally important and to determine at what grades the skills are usually taught. Sentences are not graded in the test materials. Spelling words were taken from the EDL Core Vocabularies in Reading. Item analysis and item difficulty were used in the final item selection. Sentences must be entirely correct to receive credit. Mistakes in word order can make an item incorrect. Thus, a skill not intended to be tested could result in a sentence being scored as incorrect.

Criterion-related. The following results were obtained for the Writing subtest: with the Science Research Associates (SRA) Language Arts ($n = 73$), $r = .57$ (Form A) and $r = .63$ (Form B); with the California Achievement Test ($n = 81$), $r = .37$ (Form A) and $r = .38$ (Form B); and with the Iowa Test of Basic Skills ($n = 111$), $r = .60$ (Form A) and $r = .60$ (Form B).

Construct. Results were shown to correlate with age; the Writing subtest correlates to some degree with the other subtests; it discriminates between good and poor achievers; and it correlates with grade level.

Conclusions

The validity seems sound for the QSAT Writing subtest. For those capitalization and punctuation skills tested three or more times, information for instruction could be obtained. The score obtained describes performance in all three of the areas assessed; no separate score can be obtained for spelling, capitalization, or punctuation. The standardization of the QSAT is very good, except that data on socio-economic level are needed. The test–retest reliability was somewhat low (.83), and the interval was sometimes too short, which may have resulted in an inflated correlation coefficient. Hence, additional reliability data by grade level are needed. However, results of this test would seem to be satisfactory for use in making eligibility decisions as long as the limitations noted are considered.

TEST OF ADOLESCENT LANGUAGE-2

General Description

The Test of Adolescent Language-2 (TOAL-2, 1980, 1987; written by Donald Hammill, Virginia Brown, Stephen Larsen, and J. Lee Wiederholt, and available from PRO-ED, 8700 Shoal Creek Blvd, Austin, TX 78758) was designed for students aged 12-0 to 18-5. The written expression skills assessed include Writing Vocabulary and Writing Grammar subtests. This test also contains subtests that tap skills in listening, speaking, and writing. The TOAL-2 can be group or individually administered. The administration time for the Writing Vocabulary subtest is 10–25 minutes; for Writing Grammar, it is about 15–35 minutes. Practice items are provided for each subtest, and no subtest is timed. There is one form of the TOAL-2. Basals are defined as five consecutive correct responses and ceilings as three errors in five responses. Scores are reported in terms of standard scores for subtests (mean of 10, standard deviation of 3) and for the Writing Composite (mean of 100, standard deviation of 15). Test materials include an examiner's manual, a student booklet, a student answer booklet, and a profile sheet. The new edition of the test is easier to take than the 1980 version because items were added to the lower levels.

Description of Subtests

Writing Vocabulary

This subtest consists of 30 items. The student is asked to write a sentence using a word given by the examiner. Students must be able to read each of the words. Penalities in scoring are not given for incorrect spelling or grammar.

Writing Grammar

There are 30 items on this subtest. The student is asked to read several sentences that must be combined into one written sentence.

The scoring for both of these subtests is somewhat subjective; to help with scoring, samples are provided in the manual for examiners to use as practice.

Technical Adequacy

Standardization

The number of students in the sample per age level ranged from 110 to 536. Demographic variables corresponded closely to the 1985 U.S. census data in terms of sex, geographic distribution, race, ethnicity, and urban/rural residence. No data are given on socioeconomic level of the students.

Reliability

Test–retest. A 2-week retest interval was used with 52 students 11–14 years of age. Correlations were as follows: Writing Vocabulary, .90; Writing Grammar, .87; and Writing Quotient, .98. Data are not reported by age level.

Internal consistency. Coefficient alphas exceeded .85 for the subtests, except for age 12 for Writing Vocabulary where the correlation was .84. Correlations for the Writing Composite exceeded .90 at all age levels.

Interscorer. Six raters of 100 protocols for ninth graders achieved mean correlations of .87 for the Writing Vocabulary and .98 for Writing Grammar Subtests.

Validity

Content. Written language subtests were based on various theories of language development, and field testing results were used to select the format of Writing Vocabulary. Items were selected based on results of item analysis.

Criterion-related. Three studies have examined the TOAL in terms of its relationship to results of tests of listening (Peabody Picture Vocabulary Test), speaking (Detroit Test of Learning Aptitude), and writing (Comprehensive Test of Basic Skills and Test of Written Language). For the Writing Vocabulary and Writing Grammar subtests, correlations with listening, speaking, and reading tests ranged from not significant to .63. With the tests of writing, correlations for subtests ranged from .34 to .56. For the Writing Composite, correla-

tions with tests of listening, speaking, and writing ranged from .44 to .71. With writing tests, correlations for the Writing Composite were .58 to .60.

Construct. Mean scores tend to increase with age. Written Vocabulary correlated with other subtests at from .31 to .61. The correlation with the California Short-Form Test of Academic Aptitude was .61 for Written Vocabulary and .47 for Written Grammar. Results of the TOAL have been shown to differentiate LD from retarded students, LD non-LD students, and emotionally disturbed from LD adolescents.

Conclusions

Except for the lack of data on socioeconomic levels, the standardization appears to be representative. Test–retest by age level would strengthen the technical adequacy of the test. The validity information is extensive. Hence, the TOAL-2 seems to provide useful information for use in eligibility decisions, but the limitations noted need to be considered.

TEST OF WRITTEN LANGUAGE-2

General Description

The Test of Written Language-2 (TOWL-2, 1978, 1983, 1988 written by Donald Hammill and Stephen Larsen, and available from PRO-ED, 8700 Shoal Creek Blvd, Austin, TX 78758) was designed for students aged 7-6 through 17-11. The test covers a variety of written expression skills, using both contrived and spontaneous writing formats for each area tested. Administration can be done on a group or individual basis and requires from 1.5 to 2 hours for the entire test. There are two forms (A and B). For subtests with a contrived format, a basal is defined as five consecutive correct responses and a ceiling as five consecutive errors. Results can be reported in terms of standard scores (mean of 10, standard deviation of 3) for subtests and quotients (mean of 100, standard deviation of 15) for overall results and to describe other composites. Testing materials consist of the examiner's manual, a student response booklet, and a profile form.

Description of Contrived Subtests

Vocabulary

Students are asked to write sentences using vocabulary words given by the examiner. There are 30 of these items.

Spelling and Style

These two areas are assessed by dictating sentences to students to write. There are 25 sentences, each involving at least one spelling of a word comparable with instructional grade level and the use of at least one rule for style also comparable with instructional grade level; that is, each sentence is scored for spelling *and* style. Style includes rules for both capitalization and punctuation.

For capitalization, the following rules are assessed (numbers indicate the number of items per rule):

	Form A	Form B
Beginning of sentences	25	25
Names of people	12	2
	(5 of which appear at beginning of sentences.)	
Pronoun "I"	0	3
Street	1	0
PO Box	1	0
City	0	1
State	0	1
Month	2	0
Titles	3	2
Initials	2	2
Title of publication	0	1
Special group	0	2
First word in quotation	3	0
Name of department	1	0

Punctuation rules tested follow:

Form A	Form B
Period. (20 at ends of sentences, 1 after initial in name, 5 after abbreviations and titles)	(23 at ends of sentences, 1 after initial in name, 2 after abbreviations and titles)

Form A	Form B
Question mark (5)	(2)
Comma (2 for words in series, 1 in date, 1 for appositive, 1 after name in direct address, 3 preceding quotations, 1 for a nonessential phrase, 1 to set off "no," 2 after introductory phrases, 3 for parenthetic expressions)	(3 for words in series, 1 separating city and state, 1 appositive, 1 for nonessential phrase, 2 to set off "yes," 5 after introductory phrases)
Quotation marks. (3)	(0)
Apostrophe (1 for contraction, 2 possessives)	(2) for contractions, 1 for a plural number)
Colon (0)	(2 for time)
Exclamation mark (0)	(1, plus 2 that are optional)

A comparison with the Fitzgerald list of high-frequency words indicates that students are asked to spell up to 95 different high-frequency words (i.e., 58% of the different words students are asked to spell are high-frequency words) on Form A; up to 104 (56%) are high-frequency words on Form B.

Logical Sentences

This subtest is made up of 25 items on which students are asked to rewrite sentences so that they make sense. The sentences use only words with reading levels of third grade or below, as indicated by comparison with the Harris and Jacobson word list.

Sentence Combining

There are 25 items that assess the ability to create one grammatically correct sentence from a number of short sentences.

Description of Spontaneous Subtests

The following subtests use a sample of spontaneous writing rather than a contrived format. Performance is evaluated based on a story written by the student in response to one of two pictures.

Thematic Maturity

Writing skills are assessed, including the ability "to write in a logical, sequential fashion." There are 30 criteria used to assess performance on this section.

Contextural Vocabulary

The ability to use mature words in writing is tested. "Mature" words are defined as those consisting of seven or more letters.

Syntactic Maturity

This subtest is scored based on the amount of grammatically correct material used in the spontaneous writing sample. Examiners who themselves have difficulty with grammar are likely to have problems scoring this material.

Contextual Style

Performance is assessed in terms of the number and the maturity of capitalization and punctuation rules used. "Maturity" is defined in the manual.

Contextual Spelling

The number of different words correctly spelled is the basis for assessment on this subtest.

Technical Adequacy

Standardization

There were from 82 to 132 students per age level in the normative sample for each form. The demographic characteristics of the students are similar to the 1985 U.S. census data in terms of sex, geographic distribution, race, ethnicity, and urban/rural residence. Socioeconomic level is not addressed.

Reliability

Test–retest. A 1-day to 2-week interval (mean, 2 days) was used with 77 students. The correlation for the Contrived Writing subtest was .90; for Spontaneous Writing, it was .84; and for the Overall

Written Language Quotient, it was .90. Subtest correlations ranged from .59 to .99. Hence, the Contrived Writing section and the Overall Quotient appear sufficiently reliable for use in eligibility decisions; however, data are not presented by age level. The correlation for Spontaneous Writing was somewhat low.

Alternate form. Correlations were as follows: Contrived Writing, .85; Spontaneous Writing, .78; Overall Writing Quotient, .85. Subtest correlations ranged from .61 to .77.

Interrater. This was assessed for both Form A and Form B; correlations ranged from .84 to .99.

Internal consistency. Correlations were as follows: Contrived Writing, .95; Spontaneous Writing, .94; and Overall Writing, .95. Subtest correlations ranged from .75 to .95.

Validity

Content. In terms of test structure, the conventions (e.g., rules of capitalization and punctuation), linguistic factors (e.g., vocabulary and grammar), and the ability to write logical, sequential material are all considered. Further, each of these areas is assessed using both a contrived and a spontaneous format. Thus, skills assessed appear to be appropriate and to be comprehensively tested. Item analysis was used to select items.

Numerous resources were used to develop a pool of items. For the Vocabulary subtest, words were selected from Basic Elementary Reading Vocabularies; EDL Core Vocabularies in Reading, Mathematics, Science, and Social Studies; and *A Teacher's Word Book of 30,000 Words.* For the Spelling and Style subtests, the following materials were reviewed: various scope and sequence charts, Lincoln Library of Essential Information, *Barron's How to Prepare for the New High School Equivalency Examination, The Chicago Manual of Style, The Written Word II,* and *A Dictionary of Modern English Usage.* For the subtest logical sentences, *Barron's How to Prepare for the New High School Equivalency Examination* was reviewed.

Criterion-related. Correlations with the SRA Achievement Series for Language Arts ranged from nonsignificant to .70. For the Contrived Writing Composite, the correlation was .70; for Spontaneous Writing, .39; and for the Overall Quotient, .62. Correlations with ratings of three educators for 51 students ranged from nonsignificant to .61. For the Contrived Writing Composite, the correlation was .41; for Spontaneous Writing, .42; and for the Overall Quotient, .61.

Construct. Raw scores correlated .36 to .74 with age. The intercorrelations of subtests ranged from .04 to .87. LD students were shown to attain scores that were less than average on the subtests and composites. Scores correlated from .39 to .77 with grade. Median discriminating powers ranged from .24 to .85. Factor analysis showed that all subtests load on one factor (presumably written language); with use of the varimax rotation method, support was found for the Contrived and Spontaneous Composites.

Conclusions

This version of the TOWL-2 is a considerable improvement over earlier versions. It provides much more useful information and a better sample of written expression skills. It has many strengths including use of both contrived and spontaneous formats, but it is not without limitations. Though the normative samples appear to be representative, no data are given for socioeconomic level. This could be an important variable. Test–retest reliability was assessed with a very short interval and was not evaluated by age level, which may have resulted in inflated correlation coefficients. However, this is currently the most comprehensive measure of written expression available, and it appears to be technically adequate in most respects. Though administration requires a considerable amount of time, results should provide useful information to aid in eligibility decisions and to point out general areas of strength and difficulty. It is suggested in the manual that, unless a difference of 15 points is found between the contrived and spontaneous formats for a particular area, a difference in scores should not be considered of importance; that is, it is likely to be due to chance if less than 15 points.

TEST OF WRITTEN SPELLING-2

General Description

The Test of Written Spelling-2 (TWS-2, 1986; written by Stephen Larsen and Donald Hammill, and available from PRO-ED, 8700 Shoal Creek Blvd, Austin, TX 78758) was written for use with students aged 6-6 to 18-5. The time required for administration varies from 15 to 25 minutes, and it can be given individually or to groups.

There is one form of the test. A basal is defined as five consecutive correct items and a ceiling as five errors in a row. Scores can be expressed as either percentiles or quotients (mean of 100, standard deviation of 15). Test materials consist of the examiner's manual and a protocol.

Description of Subtests

Predictable Words

For this subtest, the student is asked to write up to 50 words dictated by the examiner; these are rule-governed words.

Unpredictable Words

This subtest involves up to 50 non-rule-governed words. The examiner dictates the words and the student writes them.

Technical Adequacy

Standardization

The number of subjects per age level varied from 138 to 491. The demographic characteristics of the sample closely resembled the 1985 U.S. census data in terms of sex, geographic distribution, race, ethnicity (though the percentage of Hispanic students was low), and urban/rural residence. Socioeconomic level was not addressed.

Reliability

Test–retest. A 2-week interval was employed with 140 students in grades 2 through 8. (The manual states that 160 students were tested in grades 1–8, but this is an error.) Correlation coefficients were .90 or higher for each grade level, except grade 2. At grade 2 the Unpredictable Words subtest coefficient was .86. No data are given for grades 9 through 12.

Internal consistency. Coefficients at each age level were .90 or higher.

Standard errors of measurement. Information is provided for each age level.

Validity

Content. Five popular basal spelling series (Follett, Riverside, Scott-Foresman. Silver Burdett, and Webster/McGraw-Hill) and the EDL Core Vocabularies in Reading, Mathematics, Science, and Social Studies were reviewed to create a pool of items. Both rule-governed and non-rule-governed words were selected. Item analysis was also used in item selection.

Using the Fitzgerald list of high-frequency words, 22 of the words on the Predictable Words subtest (44%) are high-frequency words and 28 (56%) of the Unpredictable Words are high-frequency words. The words "she" and "name" appear on the Unpredictable Word list, although these are usually considered rule-governed words.

Criterion-related. No studies are reported for the TWS-2. The earlier version of the TWS was compared with several tests of spelling and the following correlations were obtained: with the Durrell Analysis of Reading Difficulty .95; with the Wide Range Achievement Test, .91; with the California Achievement Test, .97; and with the Stanford Achievement Test, .78.

Construct. Scores were shown to increase with age. LD students were found to score lower on the test than non-LD students.

Conclusions

The TWS-2 samples a relatively large number of words for spelling and, especially at the lower levels, contains a rather high percentage of high-frequency words. This test has more words than other published norm-referenced tests. The technical adequacy is good, but information on socioeconomic level is lacking and test–retest data for grades 9 through 12 are needed. Hence, this appears to be a useful measure to aid in making eligibility decisions as long as the limitations of the test are considered.

WIDE RANGE ACHIEVEMENT TEST-REVISED

General Description

The Wide Range Achievement Test-Revised (WRAT-R, 1965, 1976, 1978, 1984; written by Sarah Jastak and Gary Wilkinson, and available from Jastak Associates, 1526 Gilpin Ave, Wilmington, DE 19806) is designed for ages 5-0 to 11-11 (Level I) and 12-0 to 75 (Level II).

The written expression skill tested is spelling. The WRAT-R also contains subtests for reading and math. The administration time for the Spelling subtest is 5–10 minutes. There is one form of the test. A ceiling is 10 consecutive errors. Scores can be reported as grade equivalents, percentiles, or standard scores (mean of 100, standard deviation of 15). Test materials consist of an examiner's manual and a protocol.

Description of Spelling Subtest

The student is asked to copy marks resembling letters, to write his or her name, and to write words that are dictated by the examiner. For Level I, there are 45 words; for Level II, 46 words. The items are the same as on prior versions.

Technical Adequacy

Standardization

There were 200 subjects per level in the normative sample. The demographic characteristics of the sample correspond closely to 1982 Rand McNally Atlas data in terms of sex, geographic distribution, race, and urban/rural residence. No data are provided on ethnicity or socioeconomic status.

Reliability

Test–retest. For Level I, a correlation of .97 was obtained for 81 subjects ages 7-0 to 7-5 and 10-0 to 10-5. For Level II, a correlation of .89 was obtained for 67 subjects ages 13-0 to 13-5 and 16-0 to 16-5. No retest inteval was given, and data are not given for all age levels.

Internal consistency. Correlations for the Spelling subtest range from .88 to .99.

Standard errors of measurement. Information is provided only for the age levels used for test–retest reliability.

Validity

Content. It is stated in the manual that "The content validity . . . is apparent." However, the Spelling subtest contains items that do not assess spelling, such as copying marks. It is possible for a first grader (age 6-0 to 6-5) to score within the average range (i.e., 85+ standard score) without spelling a word. Level I is made up of 67% high-frequency words according to the Fitzgerald list, while Level II contains only 28% high-frequency words.

Criterion-related. This area is not addressed for the WRAT-R.

Construct. Authors suggest construct validity is supported by the item-separation reliability data.

Conclusions

Because numerous items do not test spelling on Level I and few words are high-frequency words on Level II, there are serious problems with the WRAT-R's content validity. The standardization lacks data on ethnicity and socioeconomic level, and test–retest data are insufficient. Hence, the WRAT-R Spelling subtest cannot be recommended for use in making eligibility decisions.

WOODCOCK–JOHNSON PSYCHOEDUCATIONAL BATTERY

General Description

The Woodcock–Johnson Psychoeducational Battery (1977; written by Richard Woodcock and Mary Johnson, and available from DLM/ Teaching Resources, PO Box 4000, One DLM Park, Allen, TX 75002) was designed for use with students in grades K through 12. A variety of written expression skills are assessed on two subtests including capitalization, punctuation, and spelling. The test contains other subtests for assessing reading and arithmetic. It is administered individually and requires 15–45 minutes for the achievement section. There are practice items for the subtests. There is one form of the test. A basal is defined as five or more correct responses and a ceiling as five or more errors. Results can be reported as grade or age equivalents, percentiles, relative performance indexes (percentage of mastery predicted when reference group would perform with 90% mastery), or standard scores. Test materials consist of the manual describing development of the test, the administration manual, and the protocol.

Description of Written Language Subtests

Dictation

The student is asked to respond in writing to directions dictated by the examiner. Two items require printing a letter. Three items require printing a capital or lower-case letter. Three items require writing punctuation marks (question mark, semicolon, asterisk). One item requires writing a contraction and two writing abbreviations. The remaining items require spelling of words. Four items require spelling of irregular plurals.

Proofing

This subtest requires that a student read a sentence or short passage, determine where an error exists, and correct it verbally. Nine items require changing verb tense or form, seven require spelling, three require punctuation rules, and nine require knowledge of rules for capitalization.

Technical Adequacy

Standardization

The number of students per age level is not given. Instead, data are given for age groups. Based on these numbers, there could be more than 100 students per age level. Demographic characteristics of the sample closely correspond to the 1977 U.S. census data for sex and race, and they are similar to the 1970 census data for geographic distribution and urban/rural residence. No specific data describe socioeconomic level, and ethnicity is not addressed.

Reliability

Test–retest. No data are given in the manual.

Internal consistency. Correlations for the Dictation subtest for grades K, 1, 3, 5, 8, and 12 range from .81 to .90. For Proofing, the correlations range from .86 to .90.

Standard errors of measurement. Data are given only for grades K, 1, 3, 5, 8, and 12.

Validity

Content. Experienced teacher and curriculum consultants were consulted on item development. For the items involving spelling, 57% are high-frequency words as indicated on the Fitzgerald list. The item sample for all areas of written expression is very limited.

Criterion-related. Correlations for written language with other measures were as follows: Iowa Test of Basic Skills (ITBS), .84; Peabody Individual Achievement Test (PIAT), .78; and Wide Range Achievement Test (WRAT), .83 for 83 third graders. For 86 fifth graders, the correlations were as follows: ITBS, .80; PIAT, .76; and the WRAT, .71. For 40 12th graders, the correlations were as follows: ITBS, .74. For 75 12th graders, they were PIAT, .79; WRAT, .86.

Construct. Data are provided to show the intercorrelations among the subtests.

Conclusions

The item sample is too limited for all of the written expression skills assessed, and too few high-frequency words are included for spelling. Hence, there are serious problems with validity. Specific data on socioeconomic background and on ethnicity of the sample are lacking. The absence of data on test–retest reliability precludes use of this measure in making eligibility decisions.

Appendix B: Reviews of Criterion-Referenced Tests

CRITERIA FOR TEST REVIEWS

Field Testing

A well-developed criterion-referenced test will have been field tested to aid in the selection of items and appropriate testing procedures and materials. Hence, a manual should describe whether this was done and how extensive a process was used.

Reliability

Test–retest reliability for criterion-referenced tests can be addressed by testing each skill three or more times or by using a test–retest procedure with at least a 2-week interval.

Validity

Content validity is particulary important for a criterion-referenced test. This is addressed by a description of the item selection procedures, which usually involves a review of various curricula. The curricula reviewed should be specified. How extensively the skills are assessed, whether appropriate testing procedures are employed, and whether there are enough items (i.e., each skill tested three or more times) are important issues to consider in evaluating content validity.

COMPREHENSIVE INVENTORY OF BASIC SKILLS

General Description

This test (1983; written by Albert Brigance, and available from Curriculum Associates, 5 Esquire Rd, North Billerica, MA 01862-2589) is designed to assess skills primarily taught in grades K through 9. The written expression skills covered include handwriting; knowledge of capitalization, punctuation, and spelling rules; addressing an envelope; and writing different types of letters. Also included in the inventory are sections for readiness, speech, reading, listening, reference skills, and math. The administration time varies from about 10 minutes to several hours, depending on how much of the test an examiner chooses to use. Some sections can be administered to groups, while most of the test is to be given individually. Test materials include the examiner's manual and a protocol. For some subtests, pages in the manual may need to be copied; other easily obtainable materials may also be needed, such as an envelope for the student to address.

Description of Subtests

Spelling

A grade placement test consists of 10 words at each grade level, 1–8. Subtests for assessing skills include writing the 21 initial consonants of dictated words, writing 33 two- and three-letter blends and digraphs at the beginning of dictated words, adding 36 suffixes to base words, adding the same 36 suffixes to base words used in written sentences, adding 15 prefixes to base words, spelling number words, writing names and abbreviations for days of the week, and writing names and abbreviations for months of the year.

Writing

For the Handwriting section, the student is asked to write upper- and lower-case letters in sequence from memory; to copy a paragraph in manuscript or cursive, which is evaluated for slant, size, spacing, formation, alignment, and neatness; and to fill in a personal data form. The data form requires knowledge of name, sex, age, birthdate, address, telephone, school, grade, teacher, room, parent or guardian, whom to notify in case of emergency, family physician, and signature. Evaluation is based on accuracy of information; however, it would seem important to consider readability of information as well.

For the Sentence Writing section, the student is asked to compose sentences incorporating words given by the examiner to determine a grade placement for ability to write; the sentences increase in complexity. No criteria are given for evaluating performance.

The Capitalization section taps the following skills by having the student write capitals over printed material, where needed (numbers indicate number of items per rule): beginning of sentences, 24; names of people, 7; pronoun "I," 3; streets, 3; cities, 3; states, 3; countries, 3; days of the week, 3; holidays, 3; months, 3; titles of people, 3; initials, 4; continents, 3; bodies of water and land forms, 3; special groups, 3; government groups, 3; religious groups and nationalities, 3; first word in a quotation, 3; proper adjectives, 3; businesses and brand names, 3; historical events and periods, 3; directions as regions, 2; and ships, trains, and planes, 1.

The Punctuation section taps knowledge of the following rules by having the student add marks to printed material where they are needed: period, 10 at ends of sentences, 3 after initials for names, 3 after abbreviations or titles, 3 in quotations, 3 in decimals or dollars and cents, 3 after nonsentences, and 2 to separate parts of a bibliography; question mark, 4; exclamation mark, 2 after exclamatory word or sentence and 3 in quotations; comma, 3 for words in series, 3 in dates, 3 separating city and state, 3 after introductory word, 3 in an address, 3 separating speaker and quotation, 3 preceding a conjunction, 3 as end mark in quotation, 2 to avoid confusion, and 2 after adverb at beginning of sentence; quotation marks, 3 before and after quotation, 3 in titles and excerpts, and 3 in interrupted quotations; apostrophe, 3 in contractions, 3 for possessives, and 2 for letters and numbers; colon, 2 to introduce a list; semicolon, 2 in compound sentence and 1 in series with comma; hyphen, 2 for compound nouns and adjectives, 2 in continuing dates, and 2 in page ranges; underlining, 3 for titles of books, plays, and magazines; and parentheses, 2 to show related material.

Items are keyed to rules for examiners.

For the Addressing an Envelope section, the student is required to address an envelope using information that is given without capitals. The student must position the information correctly on the envelope.

For the Writes Letters section, the student is asked to write three letters: a personal letter, a letter requesting information, and a letter with a consumer complaint or request. Guidelines are provided for evaluating each type of letter.

Technical Adequacy

Field Testing

The Comprehensive Inventory of Basic Skills was extensively field tested by 141 professionals from 27 states and one Canadian province. The professionals are listed in the manual.

Reliability

Nearly all skills are tested at least three times.

Validity

Item selection and the grade levels at which the skills are typically taught were based on a review of nine cited basal spelling series (1980 editions or later) and various cited references on written expression. The areas of written expression that are assessed are important, and they are tested in-depth, with most skills tested at least three times. Further, the procedures used for testing are appropriate, that is, students are asked to produce the desired responses.

Though the manual indicates the grade level at which skills are typically taught, examiners must be familiar with a student's curriculum (or consult with the student's teacher) to be sure skills have or have not been taught. In other words, these levels are guides only.

The grade placements cannot be used as achievement levels for eligibility decisions because this is not a norm-referenced test. The information also cannot be used to determine placement in a spelling series because the item sample is too small and results may not correspond to the particular basal being used.

The Sentence-Writing Grade Level Placement section is not useful because it is not norm-referenced and no criteria are given for acceptable performance.

The discontinue points on the scale usually indicate to stop testing at the examiner's discretion or when three consecutive errors are made. Because students with learning problems often have unevenly developed skills, more useful results are likely to be obtained if examiners continue to test until they are certain they have tested enough to sample the student's skills adequately. The decision to stop testing should be based on prior knowledge of the student's performance and observations during testing.

Conclusions

This appears to be the most comprehensive criterion-referenced test available for assessing written expression. If the validity considerations noted are kept in mind, this inventory can provide useful information for planning individual programs.

INVENTORY OF BASIC SKILLS

General Description

This measure (1977; written by Albert Brigance, and available from Curriculum Associates, 5 Esquire Rd, North Billerica, MA 01862-2589) assesses skills taught primarily in grades K through 6. The written expression skills tested include handwriting, capitalization, punctuation, and spelling. Sections to assess readiness skills, reading, reference skills, and mathematics are also included. The test is individually administered, but sections may be given to groups. Administration time varies from 10 minutes to 2 hours, depending on how much of the test is given. There is one form of the test. Materials include the examiner's manual and a protocol. For some subtests, pages in the manual may need to be copied, and other easily obtainable materials may be needed.

Description of Subtests

Handwriting

The student is asked to write the upper- and lower-case letters of the alphabet in cursive. It is assumed that the student knows the alphabet. Accuracy is determined by examining legibility, but no criteria are given for evaluation.

Personal Data in Writing

The student is asked to complete a form in cursive (though manuscript is permitted for items other than signature). The form requires name, address, age, telephone, birthdate, school, grade, teacher, room, sex, date, name of parent or guardian, and signature. No criteria are given for evaluating this information, though checking for accuracy of information is suggested.

Capitalization

The student is asked to add capitals to written sentences that do not contain any capitals. Skills tapped are the following, usually taught in grades 1 through 4 (numbers indicate number of items): beginning of sentences, 8; names of people, 2; streets, 2; cities, 2; states, 2; countries, 2; days of the week, 2; holidays, 2; months, 2; titles of people, 2; titles of books, 2; special groups, 1; and ethnic groups, 1.

Punctuation

This section taps skills usually taught in grade 1 through 4. The student is asked to add punctuation marks to sentences that do not have any punctuation. The skills assessed include the following: period, 4 at ends of sentences, 2 after initials, and 2 after abbreviations; question mark, 4; comma, 2 in dates, and 2 separating city and state; quotation marks, 3; apostrophe, 1 contraction and 1 possessive. Items are keyed to rules for examiners.

Parts of Speech

On this section, the student is asked to identify various parts of speech that appear in written material.

Spelling

This section begins with a grade placement test; however, because this is not a norm-referenced test, these results should not be interpreted as grade equivalents. The student is then assessed on knowledge of initial consonants, initial clusters (33), suffixes (36), and prefixes (15) for spelling.

Technical Adequacy

Field Testing

This instrument was field tested with 66 teachers and other curriculum personnel from 23 schools. Additional field testing was carried out by school personnel in Boston.

Reliability

No reliability data are given, nor are many skills tested three times or more.

Validity

Only the Suffixes and Prefixes sections are referenced to curricula. The reference for both is the Spellex program. The areas of written expression assessed are important, but skills are not tested three times and the number of skills assessed is rather limited. The procedures used to test the skills are appropriate.

Though the grade levels at which skills are typically taught are indicated, examiners must either be familiar with a student's curriculum or consult with the student's teacher to be sure of which skills have been covered; these levels are only guides.

Conclusions

This inventory is not as comprehensive, nor as well developed, as the Comprehensive Inventory of Basic Skills, since the latter also taps most skills at least three times.

INVENTORY OF EARLY DEVELOPMENT

General Description

This instrument (1978; written by Albert Brigance, and available from Curriculum Associates, 5 Esquire Rd, North Billerica, MA 01862-2589) was designed to assess skills usually learned between the ages of birth to 7. The main written expression skill tapped is handwriting. Also included in the test are sections on gross and fine motor skills, self-help skills, prespeech, speech and language, general knowledge and comprehension, readiness, and early reading and math skills. Most of the test is to be given individually; however, some sections can be given to groups of children. The administration time varies from about 10 minutes to 2 hours, depending on how many sections are given. There is one form of the test. For the Manuscript Writing section, only the manual, a protocol, and paper and pencil are needed.

Description of the Manuscript Writing Section

The skills tested in this section are usually learned between the ages of 5-3 and 7-0. The criteria for evaluating handwriting on the following subtests are slant, size, spacing, formation, alignment, neatness, and line quality. Examples of correct and incorrect handwriting are given.

Prints Personal Data

For this subtest, the student is asked to print his or her full name, age, phone number, and address. If the child is only able to use cursive writing, that is acceptable. The information is scored for printing and knowledge of the information.

Prints Upper-Case Letters Sequentially

The student prints the alphabet in capital letters for this section.

Prints Lower-Case Letters Sequentially

The student prints the alphabet in lower-case letters for this section.

Prints Upper-Case Letters Dictated

The student prints capital letters dictated by the examiner; the letters are not dictated in the order of the alphabet.

Prints Lower-Case Letters Dictated

The student prints lower-case letters dictated by the examiner; the letters are not dictated in the order of the alphabet.

Prints Simple Sentences

The student is asked to write as many sentences as he or she can about himself or herself or something that is of interest. The material is scored in terms of meeting six of seven criteria: legibility, length, spacing, spelling, syntax, punctuation, and capitalization. Some criteria are vague; for instance, misspelling "should occur infrequently." It is also suggested that originality and motivation be noted, but no criteria are provided.

Technical Adequacy

Field Testing

The inventory was field tested by more than 100 professionals. The programs involved and the types of changes made as a result of the field testing are listed in the manual.

Reliability

Skills are not tested at least three times each. However, the handwriting section could be used more than once, preferably on different days, to obtain a more adequate sample of handwriting.

Validity

If the Manuscript Writing section is used more than once with a student, an adequate sample of the student's ability to print the letters of the alphabet can be obtained. However, there would not be an adequate sample on the Prints Simple Sentences subtest to draw conclusions regarding the development of skills for spelling, syntax, punctuation, and capitalization. Further, only a sample of spontaneous writing (i.e., no contrived format) is used to test these skills.

The age levels should be used only as guides; this is clearly noted in the manual.

Rather than using the discontinue level of two consecutive errors, it would be better to test until the examiner is confident that all skills have been adequately sampled. This is particulary relevant for students who are likely to have splinter skills.

Conclusions

For written expression, this inventory assesses only the ability to use manuscript handwriting; even for this area, the inventory would need to be used more than once to obtain an adequate sample of skills. A systematic informal procedure, such as the checklist for handwriting presented in Chapter 3, would provide more comprehensive and useful information.

INVENTORY OF ESSENTIAL SKILLS

General Description

This inventory (1981; written by Albert Brigance, and available from Curriculum Associates, 5 Esquire Rd, North Billerica, MA 01862-2589) was designed mainly for secondary students who require special assistance in the classroom. Written expression skills assessed include handwriting; knowledge of rules for capitalization, punctuation, and spelling; addressing an envelope; and writing various types of letters. Most of the inventory is individually administered, but sections may be given to groups of students. Administration time varies from 10 minutes to 2 hours, depending on how many sections of the inventory are given. Test materials consist of the examiner's manual and a protocol. Some sections may require copying pages from the manual or use of easily obtainable materials, such as an envelope.

Description of Subtests

Writing Manuscript and Cursive Letters

The student is asked to write the alphabet in both upper- and lower-case letters and in manuscript and cursive for this subtest. No criteria are given for scoring other than that the letters "should be legible."

Quality of Writing

The student is asked to copy a brief passage in either manuscript or cursive. The sample is evaluated in terms of slant, size, spacing, formation, alignment, and neatness. Examples of correct and incorrect handwriting are given for each of the criteria for both manuscript and cursive forms.

Sentence-Writing Level Placement

The student is given several words and asked to write a sentence using the words. There are eight levels of items, each level including two items. Criteria for scoring include only the suggestion that the sentence must be written "correctly." This is not a norm-referenced test; hence, the grade level obtained is not useful. Levels were determined on the basis of the level of the basal spelling test in which the words were taught.

Capitalization

The student is asked to add capital letters to sentences that do not contain any capitals. There are 24 items that are keyed to rules for examiners. Rules assessed are those usually taught in grades 1 thorough 5. The rules tested are as follows (numbers indicate number of items per rule): beginning of sentences, 24; names of people, 7; streets, 3; cities, 5; states, 3; countries, 4; days of the week, 3; holidays, 3; months, 3; titles of people, 3; titles of books, articles, and magazines, 3; bodies of water and land forms, 4; and special groups, 3.

Punctuation

The student is asked to add punctuation marks to sentences that do not contain any punctuation. There are 32 items that tap skills usually taught in grades 1 through 3. Items are keyed to rules for examiners. Rules tested are as follows: period, 13 at ends of sentences, 3 after initials, and 3 after abbreviations; question mark, 3; exclamation mark, 3; comma, 3 for words in series, 3 in dates, 3 separating city and state, 3 after introductory word, 3 for appositives, and 3 after names in direct address; quotation marks, 8; apostrophe, 4 contractions and 3 possessives; colon, 3 to introduce a list and 2 for time; and semicolon, 3 separating main clauses.

Addresses Envelope

The student is given information without capital letters or punctuation that is needed to address an envelope and asked to write it on an envelope. The criteria are based on legibility, whether information is located correctly on the envelope, and if no more than one error exists in capitalization and punctuation.

Letter Writing

The student is asked to write a personal letter, a letter requesting information or material, and a consumer complaint or request letter. Guidelines are given for evaluating each type of letter including format, capitalization, punctuation, and content.

Forms

The student is asked to complete a school information form and a computer base form. Other forms can be substituted such as a form for a social security number or driver's license. There are many other forms included in other sections of the inventory, such as a health evaluation form and an application for a credit card. General guidelines are provided for evaluating performance, including a list of information that the student should be able to recall and write from memory.

Spelling

This section begins with a grade-level placement. Because the inventory is not norm-referenced, and because results are unlikely to correspond to any particular basal series, this information is not likely to be useful.

The remaining subtests assess knowledge of the following skills in spelling: 21 initial consonants, 34 initial clusters, 42 suffixes, 15 prefixes, 38 number words, days of the week and their abbreviations, and months and their abbreviations.

Technical Adequacy

Field Testing

The inventory was field tested by over 100 professionals from 55 programs in 26 states and two sites in Canada. These programs and the type of information obtained from the field testing are listed in the manual.

Reliability

Except for handwriting, most skills are tested at least three times.

Validity

The areas of written expression assessed are important and, except for handwriting, are tested in-depth with most skills assessed at least three times. Further, the procedures for testing are appropriate; that is, students are asked to produce the desired responses.

Though the manual indicates the grade level at which skills are typically taught, examiners must be familiar with the student's curriculum (or consult with the student's teacher) to be sure of which skills have been taught. In other words, these levels are guides only.

Handwriting skills can be assessed more comprehensively, and with a better sample of skills, by using the checklist for assessing handwriting presented in Chapter 3.

Conclusions

Though some useful information can be obtained from this inventory with secondary-level students, the Comprehensive Inventory of Basic Skills assesses more capitalization and punctuation skills and covers skills usually taught through grade 8. The Inventory of Essential Skills covers capitalization skills usually taught only through grade 5 and punctuation skills usually taught only through grade 3. More useful information on handwriting can be obtained using the checklist in Chapter 3. The Spellmaster (see next section) provides more detailed information on spelling skills. Hence, the most useful information for written expression from this inventory is obtained from the sections on addressing an envelope and writing letters and from the forms students are asked to complete. Skills needed to complete forms are particulary important to consider for secondary-level students. The Inventory of Essential Skills includes a wide variety of forms from which examiners can choose for an assessment.

SPELLMASTER

General Description

The Spellmaster (1976, 1987; written by Claire R. Greenbaum, and available from PRO-ED, 8700 Shoal Creek Blvd, Austin, TX 78758) assesses skills usually taught in grades K through 10, but it can be used with students in higher grades who are having difficulty with these skills. The test can be given individually or to groups, and entry-level tests take about 10 minutes each. The other tests require about 20 minutes each. There is one form of each test. Materials consist of the examiner's manual, a student answer sheet, and a separate protocol for each level of the test.

Description of the Various Sections

Entry-Level Tests

There are three entry-level tests (one for regular words, one for irregular words, and one for homophones) to determine where to begin testing in each section. Words on these tests were drawn from the diagnostic tests. There are 40 words on each entry-level test, five from each of the eight levels of the diagnostic test.

Regular Words

Eight levels of the test assess phonetically regular words. Tests 1 and 2 tap words with sounds and letters that have a one-to-one correspondence. Tests 3 through 6 tap words with sounds that can be spelled in more than one way; that is, correct spelling requires both visual memory and phonic knowledge. The words are likely to have been used in reading materials. Tests 7 and 8 (and part of test 6) tap words where the correct spelling requires knowledge of rules about suffixes, syllabication, and contractions. Protocols allow examiners to specify elements that the student has learned and specific elements with which a student has difficulty. Both knowledge of spelling elements and knowledge of rules for spelling are assessed.

Irregular Words

Eight levels of tests assess knowledge of words that do not conform to spelling rules, that is, spelling demons.

Homophones

Eight levels of tests assess knowledge of homophones (e.g., bear/bare).

Technical Adequacy

Field Testing

The Spellmaster was field tested in New England with "more than 2,500 students."

Reliability

No data are given in this manual; however, the words are the same as on the previous version. For the previous version, text–retest data were collected with a 1-week interval. Correlations for the regular and irregular words were .90 or higher; for the homonyms, they were .80 or higher. Further, each element on the Regular Word section can be tested three times if enough of the levels are administered.

Validity

No information is given in the manual to indicate how words were selected. An analysis with the Fitzgerald list indicated the following with regard to use of high-frequency words:

	High-frequency words	
Regular words	#	%
Test 1 (20 words)	9	45%
Test 2 (20 words)	9	45%
Test 3 (40 words)	29	73%
Test 4 (40 words)	17	43%
Test 5 (40 words)	9	23%
Test 6 (40 words)	9	23%
Test 7 (40 words)	7	18%
Test 8 (40 words)	2	05%

Irregular words	High-frequency words	
	#	%
Test 1 (20 words)	20	100%
Test 2 (40 words)	40	100%
Test 3 (40 words)	38	95%
Test 4 (40 words)	33	83%
Test 5 (40 words)	30	75%
Test 6 (40 words)	14	35%
Test 7 (40 words)	5	13%
Test 8 (40 words)	1	03%

Homophones	High-frequency words	
	#	%
Test 1 (20 words)	19	95%
Test 2 (40 words)	33	83%
Test 3 (40 words)	24	60%
Test 4 (40 words)	25	63%
Test 5 (40 words)	14	35%
Test 6 (40 words)	14	35%
Test 7 (40 words)	5	13%
Test 8 (40 words)	11	28%

Mastery, instructional, and frustration levels are given, but no rationale is given for how these levels were determined.

Conclusions

This appears to be the most comprehensive criterion-referenced test for assessing spelling skills, particularly at the lower and middle levels of the test where many high-frequency words are tested. More information is needed to support item selection. At the upper levels, students are assessed on words that do not appear to be of critical importance. A few of the procedures for scoring are vague and need to be clarified. However, very detailed information regarding a student's spelling skills can be obtained from this test.

TEST OF WRITTEN ENGLISH

General Description

This test (1979; written by Velma Anderson and Sheryl Thompson, and available from Academic Therapy Publications, 20 Commercial Blvd, Novato, CA 94947-6191) assesses skills usually taught in grades

2 through 6. The written expression skills tested are capitalization, punctuation, and word usage. The test is given individually and takes 10–20 minutes. There is one form of the test. The materials consist of an examiner's manual and a protocol.

Description of Subtests

Capitalization

The student is asked to read nine sentences that do not contain any capitals and circle any words that need capital letters. The rules tested are as follows (numbers indicate number of items per rule): beginning of sentences, 2; names of people, 5; street, 1; cities, 2; states, 2; countries, 1; days of the week, 1; holidays, 1; months, 1; name of school, 1; titles of people, 4; initials, 2; and first word in quotation, 1.

Punctuation

A student is asked to add punctuation marks to 13 sentences that do not contain any punctuation. Items are not keyed to rules for examiners. Rules tested are as follows: period, 2 at ends of sentences, 2 after initials, and 3 after abbreviations; question mark, 1; exclamation mark, 1; comma 2 for words in series, 1 in a date, 1 separating city and state, 2 after introductory word, 1 after name in direct address, and 1 separating speaker and quotation; quotation mark, 2; apostrophe, 2 contractions and 2 possessives.

Written Expression

Several word usage skills are assessed in this section. The student is asked to write a sentence using the word "boy" and one with the word "what"; to complete sentences with words left out; to combine sentences; and to choose correct verb forms and a correct pronoun.

Paragraph Writing

The student is asked to write a paragraph given two starter sentences. The purpose of this section is to determine if the student can apply written expression skills in spontaneous writing. Only very general guidelines are provided for evaluating performance.

Technical Adequacy

Field Testing

No information is provided on field testing.

Reliability

No correlations are given for test–retest reliability, nor are most skills assessed at least three times.

Validity

No information is provided on item selection. Not many skills are covered, nor are there many items. For the Capitalization subtest, it would have been more appropriate to have the student write the capital letters needed, rather than circle the words.

Conclusions

Given the lack of information on technical adequacy and the limited number of skills assessed, this test cannot be recommended.

References

Alessi, G., & Kaye, J. H. (1983). *Behavior assessment for school psychologists*. Stratford, CT: NASP Publications Office.

Alzofon, D., Bledsoe, L., Constantini, L., Kelly, M., Orina, M., Rhodes, R., Rogoff, D., & Scott, C. (1985). *Writing for a reason course*. Castro Valley, CA: Quercus Corp.

Anderson, K. (1985). The development of spelling ability and linguistic strategies. *The Reading Teacher, 39*, 140–147.

Anderson, M., Boren, N., Caniglia, J., Howard, W., & Krohn, E. (1980). *Apple tree*. Beaverton, OR: Dormac.

Anderson, V., & Thompson, S. K. (1979). *Test of Written English*. Novato, CA: Academic Therapy Publications.

Arena, J. (1982). *Diagnostic Spelling Potential Test*. Novato, CA: Academic Therapy Publications.

Askov, E., & Peck, M. (1982). Handwriting. In H. Mitzel, J. Best, & W. Rabinowitz (Eds.), *Encyclopedia of educational research* (5th ed., pp. 764–769). New York: The Free Press.

Aulls, M. (1981). The nature and function of context during reading and writing. In V. Froese & S. Shaw (Eds.), *Research in the language arts: Language and schooling*. Baltimore: University Park Press.

Auten, A. (1983). ERIC/RCS report: Help for reluctant writers. *Language Arts, 60*, 921–926.

Bannatyne, A., & Wichiarajote, P. (1969). Relationship between writing and spelling, motor functioning and sequencing skills. *Journal of Learning Disabilities, 2*, 4–16.

Beers, C., & Beers, J. (1981). Three assumptions about learning to spell. *Language Arts, 58*, 573–580.

Berke, S. (Ed.). (1981). *English, Inc*. Westminister, MD: Reader's Digest/ Random House.

Betts, E. (1957). *Foundations of reading instruction*. New York: American Book.

Betza, R. (1987). Online: Computerized spelling checkers: Friends or Foes? *Language Arts, 64*, 438–443.

Blackwell, P., Engen, E., Fischgrund, J., & Zarcadoolas, C. (1978). *Sentences and other systems: A language and learning curriculum for hearing impaired children.* Washington, D.C.: The Alexander Graham Bell Association for the Deaf, Inc.

Blair, R. (1975). ERIC/RCS. *The Reading Teacher, 28,* 604–607.

Blake, H., & Emans, R. (1970). Some spelling facts. *Elementary English, 47,* 241–249.

Blandford, R., & Lloyd, J. (1987). Effects of a self-instructional procedure on handwriting. *Journal of Learning Disabilities, 20,* 342–346.

Bos, C. (1988). Process-oriented writing: Instructional implications for mildly handicapped students. *Exceptional Children, 6,* 521–527.

Brigance, A. (1977). *Inventory of Basic Skills.* North Billerica, MA: Curriculum Associates.

Brigance, A. (1978). *Inventory of Early Development.* North Billerica, MA: Curriculum Associates.

Brigance, A. (1981). *Inventory of Essential Skills.* North Billerica, MA: Curriculum Associates.

Brigance, A. (1983). *Comprehensive Inventory of Basic Skills.* North Billerica, MA: Curriculum Associates.

Bruck, M. (1988). The word recognition and spelling of dyslexic children. *Reading Research Quarterly, 23,* 51–69.

Burns, P. C. (1980). *Assessment and correction of language arts difficulties.* Columbus, OH: Charles E. Merrill.

Carpenter, D. (1983). Spelling error profiles of able and disabled readers. *Journal of Learning Disabilities, 16,* 102–104.

Carpenter, D., & Miller, L. (1982). Spelling ability of reading disabled, LD students and able readers. *Learning Disability Quarterly, 5,* 65–70.

Chapman, J., & Wedell, K. (1972). Perceptual motor abilities and reversal errors children's handwriting. *Journal of Learning Disabilities, 5,* 321–325.

Chomsky, C., & Halle, M. (1968). *The sound pattern of English.* New York: Harper & Row.

Cohen, L. (1969). *Evaluating structural analysis methods used in spelling books.* Unpublished doctoral dissertation, Boston University.

Cone, T., & Wilson, L. (1981). Quantifying a severe discrepancy: critical analysis. *Learning Disability Quarterly, 4,* 359–371.

Cooper, C. R. (1977). Holistic evaluation of writing. In C. R. Cooper & L. Odell (Eds.), *Evaluating writing.* Urbana, IL: National Council of Teachers of English.

Cotterell, G. (1974). A remedial approach to a spelling disability. In B. Wade & K. Wedell (Eds.), (1974). *Spelling: Task and learner* (pp. 51–55). Edgbaston, Birmingham (England): University of Birmingham.

Cranford, B., Goodman, D., Lewis, R., & Pletz, S. (1982). *Writer's handbook.* Houston: J. B. Harbor.

Cranford, B., Goodman, D., Lewis, L., & Pletz, S. (1985). *Handbook E for young writers.* Houston: J. B. Harber.

Dagenais, D., & Beadle, K. (1984). Written language: When and where to begin. *Topics in Language Disorders, 4,* 59–85.

Dale, E., & O'Rourke, J. (1976). *A living word vocabulary*. Elgin, IL: Dome.

DeHirsch, K., Jansky, J., & Langford, W. (1966). *Predicting reading failure*. New York: Harper & Row.

Deno, S. (1985). Curriculum-based measurement: The emerging alternative. *Exceptional Children, 52,* 219–232.

Deno, S. L., Marston, D., & Mirkin, P. (1982). Valid measurement procedures for continuous evaluation of written expression. *Exceptional Children, 48,* 368–371.

Deno, S. L., Marston, D., Mirkin, P. Lowry, L., Sindelar, P., & Jenkins, J. (1982). *The use of standard tasks to measure achievement in reading, spelling, and written expression: A normative and developmental study.* (Research report no. 87.) Minneapolis: Institute for Research on Learning Disabilities, University of Minnesota.

Deno, S., & Mirkin, P. K. (1977). *Data based program modification: A manual*. Reston, VA: Council for Exceptional Children.

Deno, S., Mirkin, P. K., & Chiang, B. (1982). Identifying valid measures of reading. *Exceptional Children, 49,* 36–45.

Deno, S., Mirkin, P. K., & Wesson, C. (1983). How to write effective data-based IEPs. *Exceptional Children, 16,* 99–104.

Diederick, P. B. (1974). *Measuring growth in English*. Urbana, IL: National Council of Teachers of English.

Dunn, L., & Markwardt, F. (1970). *Peabody Individual Achievement Test*. Circle Pines, MN: American Guidance Service.

Englemann, S., & Silbert, J. (1985). *Expressive writing I & II*. Tigard, Oregon: C. C. Publications.

Englert, C., & Raphael, T. (1988). Constructing well-formed prose: Process, structure, and metacognitive knowledge. *Exceptional Children, 54,* 513–520.

Evans, D. & Blackburn, F. (1983). Screening and rescreening of letter and number writing. *S.S.S.T. Progress Report III*. Olympia, WA: Washington State Department of Public Instruction.

Falk, J. S. (1979). Language acquisition and the teaching and learning of writing. *College English, 41,* 436–447.

Ferris, D. R. (1971). Teaching children to write. In P. Lamb (Ed.), *Guiding children's language learning*. Dubuque, IA: Wm. C. Brown.

Finn, P. J. (1977). Computer-aided description of mature word choices in writing. In C. Cooper & L. Odell (Eds.), *Evaluating writing: Describing, measuring, judging*. Urbana, IL: National Council of Teachers of English.

Fitzgerald, E. (1966). *Straight language for the deaf*. Washington, D.C.: The Volta Bureau.

Fitzgerald, J. (1951). *A basic life spelling vocabulary*. Milwaukee: Bruce.

Fitzsimmons, R., & Loomer, B. (1977). *Excerpts from spelling, learning and instruction—Research and practice*. Iowa State Department of Public Instruction and The University of Iowa, Iowa City.

Fokes, J. (1976). *Fokes sentence builder*. Allen, TX: DLM/Teaching Resources.

Fokes, J. (1977). *Fokes sentence builder expansion*. Allen, TX: DLM/Teaching Resources.

Fokes, J. (1982). *Fokes written language program*. Allen, TX: DLM/Teaching Resources.

Frankel, A. J. (1976). Teaching writing skills. *Journal of Applied Behavior Analysis, 9,* 334.

Freeman, E., & Sanders, T. (1987). The social meaning of literacy: Writing instruction and community. *Language Arts, 64,* 641–645.

Fry, E. (1977). Fry's readability graph: Clarifications, validity and extension to level 17. *Journal of Reading, 1977, 21,* 242–243.

Fry, E. (1980). The new instant word list. *The Reading Teacher, 34,* 284–289.

Fuchs, L., Fuchs, D., & Warren, L. (1982). *Special education practice in evaluating student progress toward goals.* (Research report no. 21.) Minneapolis: University of Minnesota. Institute for Research on Learning Disabilities.

Furner, B. (1969a). The perceptual-motor nature of learning in handwriting. *Elementary English, 46,* 1021–1030.

Furner, B. (1969b). Recommended instructional procedures in a method emphasizing the perceptual-motor nature of learning in handwriting. *Elementary English, 46,* 1021–1030.

Furner, B. (1970). An analysis of the effectiveness of a program of instruction emphasizing the perceptual-motor nature of learning in handwriting. *Elementary English, 47,* 61–69.

Gaskins, I. (1982). A writing program for poor readers and writers and the rest of the class, too. *Language Arts, 59,* 854–861.

Gentry, J. (1982). An analysis of developmental spelling in GNYS AT WRK. *The Reading Teacher, 35,* 192–200.

Gillingham, A., & Stillman, B. (1973). *Remedial training for children with specific disability in reading, spelling, and penmanship.* Cambridge, MA: Educators Publishing Service.

Golub, L. S., & Frederick, W. C. (1971). *Linguistic structures in the discourse of fourth and sixth graders.* (Technical report no. 166.) Madison, WI: University of Wisconsin, Wisconsin Research and Development Center for Cognitive Learning.

Graham, S. (1983). The effect of self-instructional procedures on LD students' handwriting performances. *Learning Disability Quarterly, 6,* 231–234.

Graham, S. (1986). A review of handwriting scales and factors that contribute to variability in handwriting scores. *Journal of School Psychology, 24,* 63–71.

Graham, S., & Freeman, S. (1986). Strategy training and teacher vs. student controlled study conditions: Effects on LD students' spelling performances. *Learning Disability Quarterly, 9,* 15–22.

Graham, S., & Harris, K. (1988). Instructional recommendations for teaching writing to exceptional students. *Exceptional Children, 54,* 506–512.

Graham, S., & Miller, L. (1986). Seven ways to study word spellings. *The Reading Teacher, 40,* 979–980.

Granowsky, A., & Dawkins, J. (1986). *Writing sentences, paragraphs, and compositions.* Cleveland: Modern Curriculum Press.

Graves, D. (1976). Research update: Handwriting is for writing. *Language Arts, 54,* 393–399.

Graves, D. (1983). *Writing: Teachers and children at work.* Exeter, NH: Heinemann Educational Books.

Greenbaum, C. R. (1987). *Spellmaster.* Austin: PRO-ED.

Greene, H. A., & Petty, W. T. (1975). *Developing language skills in the elementary schools.* Boston: Allyn & Bacon.

Guerin, G., & Maier, A. (1983). *Informal assessment in education.* Palo Alto, CA: Mayfield.

Hall, J. K. (1981). *Evaluating and improving written expression.* Boston: Allyn & Bacon.

Hammill, D. D. (1986). Correcting handwriting deficiencies. In D. D. Hammill & N. Bartel (Eds.), *Teaching students with learning and behavior problems* (4th ed.). Austin, TX: PRO-ED.

Hammill, D. D. (1987). *Assessing the abilities and instructional needs of students.* Austin, TX: PRO-ED.

Hammill, D. D., Ammer, J., Cronin, M., Mandlebaum, L., & Quinby, S. (1987). *Quick Score Achievement Test.* Austin, TX: PRO-ED.

Hammill, D. D., & Bartel, N. (1982). *Teaching children with learning and behavior problems.* Boston: Allyn & Bacon.

Hammill, D. D., Brown, L., Larsen, S., & Wiederholt, J. L. (1987). *Test of Adolescent Language-2.* Austin, TX: PRO-ED.

Hammill, D. D., & Larsen, S. (1983). *Test of Written Language.* Austin, TX: PRO-ED.

Hammill, D. D., & Larsen, S. (1988). *Test of Written Language-2.* Austin, TX: PRO-ED.

Hammill, D. D., & Leigh, J. E. (1983). *Basic School Skills Inventory-Diagnostic.* Austin, TX: PRO-ED.

Hammill, D. D., & Poplin, M. (1982). Problems in written composition. In D. D. Hammill & N. R. Bartel (Eds.), *Teaching children with learning and behavior problems.* Boston: Allyn & Bacon.

Hanna, P., Hanna, J., Hodges, R., & Rudolf, E. (1966). *Phoneme-grapheme correspondence as cues to spelling improvement.* Washington, DC: U.S. Government Printing Office, U.S. Office of Education.

Harris, K., & Graham, S. (1985). Improving learning disabled students' composition skills: Self-control strategy training. *Learning Disability Quarterly, 8,* 27–36.

Henderson, E. (1974). Correct spelling—An inquiry. *The Reading Teacher, 27,* 176–179.

Henderson, E. (1985). *Teaching spelling.* Boston: Houghton-Mifflin.

Hermreck, L. A. (1979). *A comparison of the written language of LD and non-LD elementary children using the inventory of written expression and spelling.* Unpublished master's thesis, University of Kansas, Lawrence, KS.

Hillerich, R. (1978). *A writing vocabulary of elementary children.* Springfield, IL: Charles C. Thomas.

Hillerich, R. (1985). *Teaching children to write, K-8.* Englewood Cliffs, NJ: Prentice-Hall.

Hillocks, G. (1987). Synthesis of research on teaching writing. *Educational Leadership, 44,* 73–82.

Hirshoren, A. (1969). A comparison of the predictive validity of the revised Stanford–Binet Intelligence Scale and the Illinois Test of Psycholinguistic Ability. *Exceptional Children, 35,* 517–521.

Hodges, R. (1981). The language base of spelling. In V. Froese & S. Straw (Eds.), *Research in the language arts*. Baltimore: University Park Press.

Hodges, R. (1982). Research update on the development of spelling ability. *Language Arts, 59,* 284–290.

Hunt, K. W. (1965). *Grammatical structures written at three grade levels.* (NCTE research report no. 3.) Champaign, IL: National Council of Teachers of English.

Jastak, S., & Wilkinson, G. (1984). *Wide Range Achievement Test-Revised.* Wilmington: Jastak Associates, Inc.

Johnson, D., & Myklebust, H. (1967). *Learning disabilities: Educational principles and practices.* New York: Grune & Stratton.

Johnson, T., Langford, K., & Quorn, K. (1981). Characteristics of an effective spelling program. *Language Arts, 58,* 581–588.

Kaufman, A., & Kaufman, N. (1985). *Kaufman Test of Educational Achievement.* Circle Pines, MN: American Guidance Service.

Kean, J. (1981). Grammar: A perspective. In V. Froese & S. Straws (Eds.) *Research in the language arts*. Baltimore: University Park Press.

King, D. (1986). *Keyboarding skills: All grades.* Cambridge, MA: Educators Publishing Service.

Koenke, K. (1986). Handwriting instruction: What do we know? *The Reading Teacher, 36,* 214–216.

Kosiewicz, M., Hallahan, D., Lloyd, J., & Graves, A. (1982). Effects of self-instruction and self-correction procedures on handwriting performances. *Learning Disability Quarterly, 5,* 71–78.

Larsen, S. C. (1987). Assessing writing. In D. D. Hammill (Ed.), *Assessing the abilities and instructional needs of students.* Austin: PRO-ED.

Larsen, S., & Hammill, D. D. (1986). *Test of Written Spelling-2.* Austin: PRO-ED.

Lehr, F. (1984). Spelling instruction: Phonics, rules, and word lists. *The Reading Teacher, 38,* 218–220.

Lesiak, J. (1984). Review of a multisensory approach to language arts for specific language disability children. *Techniques, 1,* 7–13.

Lesiak, J., Lesiak, W., & Kirchheimer, J. (1979). Auditory and visual factors related to spelling success. *Psychology in the Schools, 16,* 491–494.

Lewis, E. R., & Lewis, H. P. (1965). An analysis of errors in the formation of manuscript letters by first grade children. *American Educational Research Journal, 2,* 25–35.

Lloyd-Jones, R. (1977). Primary trait scoring. In C. R. Cooper & L. Odell (Eds.), *Evaluating writing: Describing, measuring, judging.* Urbana, IL: National Council of Teachers of English.

Mann, P., Suiter, P., & McClung, R. (1979). *Handbook in diagnostic and prescriptive teaching.* Boston: Allyn & Bacon.

Marzano, R. J., & DiStefano, P. (1978). *Five empirically based composition skills.* ERIC Document Reproduction Service, ED 162 337.

Moran, M. R. (1981). Performance of learning disabled and low achieving secondary students on formal features of a paragraph-writing task. *Learning Disability Quarterly, 4,* 271–280.

Morris, N. T., & Crump, W. D. (1982). Syntactic and vocabulary development in the written language of learning disabled and nonlearning disabled students at four age levels. *Learning Disabilities Quarterly, 5,* 163–172.

Moseley, D. (1974). Some cognitive and perceptual correlates of spelling ability. In B. Wade & K. Wedell (Eds.), *Spelling: Task and learner* (pp. 15–22). Birmingham, England: University of Birmingham.

Myklebust, H. (1973). *Development and disorders of written language: Studies of normal and exceptional children* (Vol. 2). New York: Grune & Stratton.

Naidoo, S. (1972). *Specific dyslexia.* London: Pitman.

Newcomer, P., & Bryant, B. (1986). *Diagnostic Achievement Test for Adolescents.* Austin: PRO-ED.

Newcomer, P., & Curtis, D. (1984). *Diagnostic Achievement Battery.* Austin: PRO-ED.

Newland, T. E. (1932). An analytical study of the development of illegibilities in handwriting from the lower grades to adulthood. *Journal of Educational Research, 26,* 249–258.

Nichols, A. (1949). The analysis and correction of spelling difficulties. *Elementary School Journal, 50,* 154–161.

Nolen, P. (1980). Sound reasoning in spelling. *The Reading Teacher, 33,* 538–543.

Odom, R. R. (1964). Growth of a language skill: Punctuation. *California Journal of Educational Research, 13,* 12–17.

O'Donnell, R. C., Griffin, W. J., & Norris, R. C. (1967). *Syntax of kindergarten and elementary school children: A transformational analysis.* (NCTE research report no. 8.) Urbana, IL: National Council of Teachers of English.

Packard, D., & Rybicki, V. (1983). *Teaching resources spelling series.* Allen, TX: DLM/Teaching Resources.

Page, E. B. (1968). The use of the computer in analyzing student essays. *International Review of Education, 14,* 210–225.

Partoll, S. (1976). Spelling demonology revisited. *Academic Therapy, 11,* 339–348.

Phelps-Gunn, T., & Phelps-Terasaki, D. (1982). *Written language instruction: Theory and remediation.* Rockville, MD: Aspen Systems Corp.

Poteet, I. (1980). Informal assessment of written expression. *Learning Disabilities Quarterly, 3,* 88–98.

Poplin, M. S., Gray, R., Larsen, S., Banikowski, A., & Mehring, T. (1980). A comparison of written expression abilities in learning disabled and non-learning disabled students in three grade levels. *Learning Disabilities Quarterly, 3,* 46–53.

Poteet, J. A. (1979). Characteristics of written expression of learning disabled and non-learning disabled elementary-school students. *Diagnostique, 4,* 60–74.

Psychological Corporation (1983). *Basic Achievement Skills Individual Screener.* San Antonio, TX: Author.

Rowell, C. (1975). Don't throw away those spelling test papers . . . yet! *Elementary English, 52,* 253–257.

Russell, D. (1955). A second study of characteristics of good and poor spellers. *Journal of Educational Psychology, 46,* 129–141.

Salvia, J., & Ysseldyke, J. (1981). *Assessment in special and remedial education.* Boston: Houghton Mifflin.

Schell, L. (1975). B+ in composition: C– in spelling. *Elementary English, 52,* 239–242, 257.

Schlagel, R. (1982). *A qualitative inventory of word knowledge: A developmental study of spelling, grades one through six.* Unpublished doctoral dissertation, University of Virginia, Charlottesville.

Shapiro, E. S. (1987). *Behavioral assessment in school psychology.* Hillsdale, NJ: Lawrence Erlbaum.

Shapiro, E. S., & Lentz, F. E. (1986). Behavioral assessment of academic skills. In T. R. Kratochwill (Ed.), *Advances in school psychology.* Hillsdale, NJ: Lawrence Erlbaum.

Slingerland, B. (1971). *A multisensory approach to language arts for specific language disability children: A guide for primary teachers.* Cambridge, MA: Educators Publishing Service.

Slingerland, B. (1976). *Basics in scope and sequence of a multisensory approach to language arts for specific language arts for specific language disability children: A guide for primary teachers in the second-year continuum.* Cambridge: Educators Publishing Service.

Slingerland, B. (1981). *A multisensory approach to language arts for specific language disability children: A guide for elementary teachers.* Cambridge, MA: Educators Publishing Service.

Slingerland, B., & Aho, M. (1985a). *Learning to use cursive handwriting.* Cambridge, MA: Educators Publishing Service.

Slingerland, B., & Aho, M. (1985b). *Learning to use manuscript handwriting.* Cambridge, MA: Educators Publishing Service.

Spache, G. (1940). Characteristic errors of good and poor spellers. *Journal of Educational Research, 34,* 182–189.

Starlin, C. M. (1982). On reading and writing. *Iowa Monograph Series.* Des Moines, IA: Department of Public Instruction.

Stoddard, B. (1987). Teaching writing to learning-disabled students. *The Pointer, 32,* 14–18.

Straw, S. (1981). Grammar and teaching of writing: Analysis versus synthesis. In V. Froese & S. Straw (Eds.), *Research in the language arts: Language and schooling.* Baltimore: University Park Press.

Strong, W. (1986). *Creative approaches to sentence combining.* Urbana, IL: National Council of Teachers of English, ERIC.

Strunk, W., & White, E. B. (1972). *The elements of style.* New York: Macmillan Publishing Company.

Taylor, S., Frackenpohl, H., White, C., Nieririda, B., Browning, C., & Birsner, E. (1979). *EDL core vocabularies in reading, mathematics, science, and social studies.* New York: EDL/Arista.

Thomas, C. C., Englert, C. S., & Gregg, S. (1987). An analysis of errors and strategies in the expository writing of learning disabled students. *Remedial and Special Education, 8,* 21–30.

Thurber, D. (1978). *D'Nealian handwriting.* Glenview, IL: Scott Foresman & Co.

Thurber, D. (1981). *D'Nealian handwriting.* Glenview, IL: Scott Foresman & Co.

Thurber, D. (1987). *D'Nealian handwriting.* Glenview, IL: Scott Foresman & Co.

Trocki, P. (1985). *Spelling workout.* Cleveland: Modern Curriculum Press.

Venezky, R. (1967). English orthography: Its graphical structure and its relation to sound. *Reading Research Quarterly, 2,* 75–105.

Wallace, G., Cohen, S., & Polloway, E. A. (1987). *Language arts.* Austin: PRO-ED.

Wallace, G., & Larsen, S. (1978). *Educational assessment of learning problems: Testing for teaching.* Boston: Allyn & Bacon.

Weiner, E. S. (1980a). The diagnostic evaluation of writing skills (DEWS): Application of DEWS criteria to writing samples. *Learning Disability Quarterly, 3,* 54–59.

Weiner, E. S., (1980b). Diagnostic evaluation of writing skills. *Journal of Learning Disabilities, 13,* 43–48.

Whitt, J., Paul, P., & Reynolds, C. (1988). Motivate reluctant learning disabled writers. *Teaching Exceptional Children, 54,* 37–39.

Wittels, H., & Greisman, J. (1982). *How to spell it.* New York: Grosset & Dunlap.

Woodcock, R., & Johnson, M. (1977). *Woodcock-Johnson Psychoeducational Battery* (pp. 921–926). Allen, TX: DLM/Teaching Resources.

Ysseldyke, J., & Christenson, S. L. (1987). *The Instructional Environment Scale.* Austin, TX: PRO-ED.

Index